A Grief
Sanctified

A Grief Sanctified

Passing Through Grief to Peace and Joy

J.I. Packer

PRESENTS RICHARD BAXTER'S MEMOIR OF
HIS WIFE'S LIFE AND DEATH

SERVANT PUBLICATIONS
ANN ARBOR, MICHIGAN

Vine Books is an imprint of Servant Publications especially designed to serve
evangelical Christians.

Published by Servant Publications
P.O. Box 8617
Ann Arbor, Michigan 48107

Cover design: Brian Fowler, DesignTeam, Grand Rapids, MI

98 99 00 10 9 8 7 6 5 4 3 2

Printed in the United States of America
ISBN 0-89283-841-8

For Monty and Rosemary
and for Kit
again

Contents

Prologue

To the Reader

Grief

THIS IS A BOOK FOR CHRISTIAN PEOPLE about six of life's realities—love, faith, death, grief, hope, and patience. Centrally it is about grief.

What is grief? It can safely be said that everyone who is more than a year old knows something of grief by firsthand experience, but a clinical description will help us to get it in focus. Grief, then, is the inward desolation that follows the losing of something or someone we loved—a child, a relative, an actual or anticipated life partner, a pet, a job, one's home, one's hopes, one's health, or whatever.

Loved is the key word here. We lavish care and affection on what we love and those whom we love, and when we lose the beloved, the shock, the hurt, the sense of being hollowed out and crushed, the haunting, taunting memory of better days, the feeling of unreality and weakness and hopelessness, and the lack of power to think and plan for the new situation can be devastating.

Grief may be mild or intense, depending on our own emotional makeup and how deeply we invested ourselves in relating to the lost reality. Ordinarily, the most acute griefs are felt at times of bereavement, when old guilts and neglects come back to mind, and thoughts of what we could and should have done differently and better come hammering at our hearts like battering rams. When Shakespeare's Romeo said, "He jests at scars, that never felt a wound," he was thinking of the pangs of eros, but his words apply equally to the pangs of grief. Grief is thus, as we say, no laughing matter; in the most profound sense, it is just the reverse.

Bereavement, we said—meaning the loss through death of someone we loved—brings grief in its most acute and most disabling form, and coping with such grief is always a struggle. Bereavement becomes a supreme test of the quality of our faith. Faith, as the divine gift of trust in the triune Creator-Redeemer, the Father, the Son, and the Holy Spirit, and so as a habit implanted in the Christian heart, is meant to act as our gyroscopic compass throughout life's voyage and our stabilizer in life's storms; but bereavement shakes unbelievers and believers alike to the foundations of their being, and believers no less than others regularly find that the trauma of living through grief is profound and prolonged. The idea, sometimes voiced, that because Christians know death to be for believers the gate of glory, they will therefore not grieve at times of bereavement is inhuman nonsense.

Grief is the human system reacting to the pain of loss, and as such it is an inescapable reaction. Our part as Christians is not to forbid grief or to pretend it is not there, but to maintain humility and practice doxology as we live through it. Job is our model here. At the news that he had lost all his wealth and that his children were dead, he got up and tore his robe and shaved his head. Then he fell to the ground in worship and said, "Naked I came from my mother's womb, and naked I shall depart. The Lord gave and the Lord has taken away; may the name of the Lord be praised" (Job 1:21). Managing grief in this way is, however, easier to talk about than to do; we are all bad at it, and for our own times of grieving we need all the help we can get.

At the heart of Richard Baxter's grief book is an object lesson in what we may properly call grief management. Here we shall meet a grieving husband memorializing the soulmate whom, after nineteen years of marriage, he had tragically lost less than a month before. Margaret Baxter died at age forty-five after eleven days of delirium, her reason having almost wholly left her, as she had long feared it might do. A starvation diet had weakened her, and the barbarous routine of bloodletting, the universal seventeenth-century remedy for all disorders, had done her the reverse of good. A modern reader might guess that menopausal troubles were involved in her decline, but in her day the medical realities of menopause were unknown country.

Richard, her husband, twenty years older and a knowledgeable amateur physician, thought it was what she took over a period of time for her health ("Barnet waters" from Barnet spa north of London, and "too much tincture of amber") that brought on her death.[1] "In depth of grief,"[2] "under the power of melting grief,"[3] Baxter resolved to write her life, and within days produced a gem of Christian biography, at once a lover's tribute to his fascinating though fragile mate and a pastor's celebration of the grace of God in a fear-ridden, highly strung, oversensitive, painfully perfectionist soul. Baxter's narrative is a classic of its kind and will help us in all sorts of ways.[4]

In 1681, when Richard wrote this "Breviate" (meaning "short account") of Margaret's life, he was probably the best known, and certainly the most prolific, of England's Christian authors. Already in the 1650s, when despite chronic ill health he masterminded a tremendous spiritual surge in his small-town parish of Kidderminster, he had become a best-selling author and had produced enough volumes of doctrine, devotion, and debate to earn himself the nickname "scribbling Dick." Debarred in 1662 from parochial ministry by the unacceptable terms on which the Act of Uniformity reestablished the Church of England, he made writing his main business, and by 1680, when he reached sixty-five, he had over ninety publications to his name.

Then within six months came four bereavements.

In December 1680 "our dear friend" John Corbet, also an ejected minister and a close comrade of forty years' standing, who with his wife had lived in the Baxters' home from 1670 to 1672, died. Baxter's funeral sermon for Corbet testifies to their affection for each other,[5] as did Margaret's immediate persuasion of his widow to move back into the Baxter home on a permanent basis to be her personal companion.

Next, two members of what Richard called his "ancient family" finished their course: Mary, his stepmother, his father's second wife, who had been living with them for a decade and had reached her mid-nineties, and "my old friend and housekeeper, Jane Matthews," who had presided over his bachelor parsonage in Kidderminster and was now in her late seventies.

Finally on June 14, 1681, Margaret's own life ended. As a pastor Baxter was, of course, used to dealing with deaths, but the cumulative strain of these four losses must have been considerable.

It should not surprise us that the distressed widower turned to a literary project for consolation and relief. He wrote very easily, and the writer's discipline of getting things into shape is always therapeutic at times of emotional strain. Margaret's will had called for a new edition of Baxter's funeral sermon for Mary Hanmer (formerly Charlton), Margaret's own mother, and Baxter's first thought was to bring out a volume in which he would prefix to that sermon four "breviates"—short lives of Mary Hanmer, Mary Baxter, Jane Matthews, and Margaret, all together. Friends, however, persuaded him to drop the first three and cut out many personal details from his draft of the life of Margaret. "He was 'loath to have cast by' these 'little private Histories of mine own Family,' but he was 'convinced' by his friends ... that his love and grief had led him to overestimate the value to others of what affected him so nearly."[6] Much, therefore, that we late-twentieth-century romantics, with our almost indecent interest in private lives, would like to know about "the occasions and inducements of [their] marriage" is lost to us. Nonetheless, the Breviate that finally emerged "is undoubtedly the finest of Baxter's biographical pieces,"[7] and one hopes that writing it benefited him as much as reading it can benefit us.

The personal memoir with a spiritual focus, a literary category pioneered by Athanasius' *Life of Antony* and Augustine's *Confessions,* was much more in evidence among the people of the Reformation after the mid-sixteenth century, Beza's *Life of Calvin* and the stories of the martyrs in Foxe's *Acts and Monuments* being among the more impressive examples. The seventeenth-century fashion of writing "characters"—literary profiles of human types and of particular individuals, viewed in lifestyle terms—further honed Puritan biographical skills; and Baxter's Breviate, though low-key and matter-of-fact in style, is Puritan spiritual storytelling at its best: storytelling that is made more poignant by Richard's intermittent unveiling of his grief as he goes along. More will be said about this in due course.

C.S. Lewis's Grief Book

"Mere Christianity"—meaning historic mainstream Bible-based discipleship to Jesus Christ, without extras, omissions, diminutions, disproportions, or distortions—was Baxter's own phrase for the faith he held and sought to spread. Three centuries after his time, C.S. Lewis used the same phrase as a title for the 1952 book in which he put together three sets of broadcast talks on Christian basics. Probably Lewis got the phrase from Baxter,[8] and certainly in likening what he offered to the shared hallway off which open the rooms of the various denominational heritages[9] he was saying something very Baxterish. Lewis and Baxter belong together as men with a common purpose as well as a common faith.

Now Lewis, like Baxter, also lost his wife in his sixties, and while in the grip of grief turned to writing—the end product being his justly admired *A Grief Observed*. "After her [his wife's] death in July 1960," wrote Lewis' friend and biographer George Sayer, "he felt both paralyzed and obsessed.... To liberate himself, he did what he had done in the past—he wrote a book about it, a book that is very short and desperately truthful.... In it he is trying to understand himself and the nature of his feelings. It is analytical, cool, and clinical."[10]

Baxter too is analytical, cool, and clinical, but about Margaret rather than himself, and this sets the two books in interesting contrast. Lewis' "breviate" of his bereavement experience has been widely seen as a model for Christian grief-narrative books, several of which have appeared in recent years,[11] and this gives the contrast significance as well as interest. We shall reflect on this contrast in our final section.

For the moment, however, C.S. Lewis must wait in the wings. It is Richard and Margaret Baxter who stand center stage. Our introduction has done its job of introducing, and now we must move on to where our story really starts.

Part One

Great Gladness:
Margaret With Richard

Two Puritans

Richard (1615-91), evangelist, pastor, and tireless writer of devotional and controversial theology, and Margaret (1636-81), his wife, were Puritans.

That means they were gloomy, censorious English Pharisees, who wore black clothes and steeple hats, condemned all cheerfulness, hated the British monarchy, and wanted the Church of England and its Book of Common Prayer abolished—right?

Wrong—off track at every point! Start again.

Richard and Margaret came of land-owning families. Adult members of these families were called gentlemen and gentlewomen; they formed England's aristocracy, as distinct from England's laborers, tradesmen, and professionals (lawyers, physicians, clergy, and educators). Richard's father, Richard Baxter senior, was a very minor gentleman, with a small, debt-laden estate at Eaton Constantine in Shropshire. Margaret's father, Francis Charlton, Esquire, was a more significant gentleman, a leading justice of the peace and a wealthy man. Margaret grew up in his home, Apley Castle, less than four miles from Eaton Constantine. One of the traumas of her childhood was the demolition of the castle by Royalist troops in 1644, during the Civil War.[1]

Richard Baxter

Richard first met Margaret when she came to Kidderminster (in Worcestershire, next county to Shropshire) to live with her godly mother, now Mrs. Hanmer, who having been widowed a second time had moved there to get the benefit of Richard's magnificent ministry. Kidderminster was an artisan community of some eighteen hundred adults, with weaving as its cottage industry. Half the town crowded into church every Sunday, and many hundreds had professed conversion.

Margaret Charlton

Margaret was a frivolous, worldly minded teenager when she arrived, and at first she disliked both the town and the piety of its inhabitants. But a sermon series on conversion which Baxter preached in 1657 set her seeking a change of heart and a total commitment to devoted, penitent, Christ-centered worship and service of God. In due course she found herself assured of her sincerity in this commitment, and thus of her new birth, pardon for sin, and title to glory, and eagerly she took her place among

Baxter's working-class converts. But then she sickened, and for months seemed to be mortally ill with lung problems that nothing would relieve. Special intercession with fasting for her life by Baxter and his inner circle of prayer warriors resulted, however, in a sudden cure "as it were by nothing"—a healing which today would be called miraculous, and was one of several such in Kidderminster in Baxter's time.[2]

Mrs. Hanmer's home was a large war-damaged house alongside the churchyard, where she "lived as a blessing amongst the honest poor weavers, ... whose company for their piety she chose before all the vanities of the world."[3] It is clear that Pastor Richard was often in her home, and Margaret, who found it difficult to discuss her spiritual problems with her mother, depended heavily on him for what we would call spiritual direction. One thing led to another, and when in April 1660, straight after the day of thanksgiving for Margaret's healing,[4] he left for London for an indefinite period to play his part in the forthcoming restoration of the Church of England,[5] she found herself wanting to follow him. Soon her mother and she had relocated in London, where Mrs. Hanmer died of fever in 1661.

Baxter omitted from his memoir of Margaret "the occasions and inducements of our marriage,"[6] but it is not hard to put two and two together. By the end of 1661 Baxter, who had always urged that the combined claims of marriage and parish were more than any clergyman could really meet, knew that his Kidderminster ministry was over, that there was no prospect of future parochial ministry for him,[7] and thus that his case for clerical celibacy no longer applied to himself. Facing a future in which he expected writing to be his main ministry, he needed a home and someone to look after both him and it—for, by his own admission, he knew little of matters domestic and did not want to be bothered with them.

Meantime, now that her mother was dead, Margaret was alone in the world, and it seems clear that she knew she wanted to be Baxter's wife, just as more than a century before Katherine von Bora had wanted to be Luther's. It is a natural guess that Mrs. Hanmer had seen this and let it be known that she would like it to happen. Who knows what she said to Baxter when he was with her in what from the start she expected to be her last illness? At all events, an official license was issued on April 29, 1662, and the ceremony took place on September 10, after "many changes ... stoppages ... and long delays."[8] There followed nineteen years of happy life together, till Margaret died.

And what about Puritanism? Both were confessedly Puritans to their fingertips, but what did that mean? The Puritanism of history was not the barbarous, sourpuss mentality of time-honored caricature, still less the heretical Manicheism (denial of the goodness and worth of created things and everyday pleasures) with which some scholars have identified it. It was, rather, a wholistic renewal movement within English-speaking Protestantism, which aimed to bring all life—personal, ecclesiastical, political, social, commercial; family life, business life, professional life—under the didactic authority and the purging and regenerating power of God in the gospel to the fullest extent possible. This meant praying and campaigning for thorough personal conversion, consecration, repentance, self-knowledge, and self-discipline; for more truth and life in the preaching, worship, fellowship, pastoral care, and disciplinary practice of the churches; for dignity, equity, and high moral standards in society; for philanthropy, generosity, and a good-Samaritan spirit in face of the needs of others; and for the honoring of God in home life through shared prayer and learning of God's truth, maintaining decency, order, and love, and practising "family government" (a Puritan tag phrase) according to the Scriptures.

The "heart-work" that was central to Puritan piety—self-examination, self-condemnation, self-motivation, self-dedication, and the continual focusing of faith, hope, and love on the Lord Jesus Christ—had nothing morbid or self-absorbed about it; it was simply the inner reality of disciplined devotion. As Baxter himself never tired of urging, cheerfulness and joy—set in a frame of faith, humility, watchfulness, and obedience ("duties")—are of the essence of the true Christian life. This was the Puritanism that Richard and Margaret sought to live out.[9]

Puritan Marriage

The Puritans called for the sanctifying of all relationships as an integral part of one's service of God. The rule for sanctifying anything was Scripture. What did this mean for marriage? What was the Puritan ideal for holy wedlock? "The serious divine Richard Baxter is united in marriage to a young Puritan lady of aristocratic birth, a woman of fine mind, deep spiritual experience and kindred Puritan sympathy."[10] What did they understand themselves to be taking on?

The question is not hard to answer, for the evidence is plentiful and homogeneous.[11] Abundant printed treatises and wedding sermons all tell the same story. The Puritans do not appear as post-Christian moderns whose thinking stops short at physical attraction, sexual satisfaction, and parental fulfillment (cuddles, orgasms, and babies, to put it bluntly). Nor do they appear as Victorian sentimentalists, dwelling entirely on the beauty of rose-colored rapport between souls, with bodies right out of the picture. W.J. Wilkinson sounds very Victorian when he writes of Richard and Margaret as "two souls who love God and love each other with that sublime, spiritual beauty in which souls are wed, which gives orientation to life and is eternal,"[12] and quotes Browning to ram the idea home.

To be sure, there is real truth in the Victorian vision, just as there is real truth in the physicality of the modern conception, but neither perspective is theological enough to find the Puritan wavelength.

Nor, again, do the Puritans appear as eighteenth-century evangelicals, ruthlessly denying that the "foolish passion which the world calls *love*" should influence the godly man's choice of a wife.[13] "I know you must have love to those that you match with," writes Baxter, and his only proviso is that it must be "rational" love that discerns "worth and fitness" in its object, as distinct from "blind ... lust or fancy."[14]

So how, in positive terms, did the Puritans conceive of marriage? They saw it as a gift, a calling, a task, and a lifelong discipline, and programmed themselves for it accordingly. What this meant is well shown us in Richard's own monumental *Christian Directory*, to which we now turn.

First published as a three-inch-thick folio in 1673, this work is rather more than a million words long. Its title page reads thus: *A Christian Directory: or A Sum of Practical Theology, and Cases of Conscience. Directing Christians How to Use their Knowledge and Faith; How to Improve all Helps and Means, and to Perform all Duties; How to Overcome Temptations, and to Escape or Mortify Every Sin. In Four Parts. I. Christian Ethics (or Private Duties). II. Christian Economics (or Family Duties). III. Christian Ecclesiastics (or Church Duties). IV. Christian Politics (or Duties to our Rulers and Neighbors).* (As we plow through this, we should remember that in the days before dust jackets and blurbs, title pages had to be fulsome, since it was only there that information as to what you would find in the book if you bought it could be given.)

Richard's *magnum opus* should be better known than it is, for it is truly a landmark, a full-scale compendium of Puritan moral and practical theology in all its many-sided devotional, pastoral, life-embracing, and community-building strength. Part II of this magisterial distillation of Puritan wisdom is subtitled "The Family Directory, Containing Directions for the True Practice of All Duties Belonging to Family Relations, with the Appurtenances,"[15] and here Richard discusses, among other things, first, how a man should determine before God whether and whom to marry, and second, the "duties" (mutual obligations) of husband and wife within the marriage relationship. These sections are of special interest not only because Baxter is here creaming off the wisdom of a century of Puritan discussion as tested and verified in a busy fifteen-year pastorate, but because he wrote them in 1664-65, two or three years into his own marriage, the experience of which was bound to color his thinking to some extent. What, now, does he have to say?

"Marriage," declares the Westminster Confession, XXI:2, "was ordained for the mutual help of husband and wife, for the increase of mankind with a legitimate issue, and of the church with a holy seed, and for preventing of uncleanness." Baxter assumes this throughout. Who then should marry? Minors for whom marriages were arranged by their parents;[16] persons with incontinent hearts, as directed in 1 Corinthians 7:9;[17] and any in whose case it appears "that in a married state, one may be most serviceable to God and the public good."[18] But go into it with your eyes open! "Rush not into a state of life, the inconveniences of which you never thought on."[19] Baxter lists twenty "inconveniences," of which the most striking are these:

- Marriage ordinarily plungeth men into excess of worldly cares....

- Your wants in a married state are hardlier supplied, than in a single life.... You will be often at your wit's end, taking thought for the future....

- Your wants in a married state are far hardlier borne than in a single state. It is far easier to bear personal wants ourselves, than to see the wants of wife and children: affection will make their sufferings pinch you.... But especially the discontent and impatiences of your family will more discontent you than all their wants....

- By that time wife and children are provided for, and all their importunate desires satisfied, there is nothing considerable left for pious or charitable uses. Lamentable experience proclaimeth this....

- And it is no small patience which the natural imbecility [weakness] of the female sex requireth you to prepare.... Women are commonly of potent fantasies, and tender, passionate, impatient spirits, easily cast into anger, or jealousy, or discontent.... They are betwixt a man and a child.... And the more you love them, the more grievous it will be, to see them still [constantly] in discontents....

- And there is such a meeting of faults and imperfections on both sides, that maketh it much the harder to bear the infirmities of others aright.... Our corruption is such, that though our intent be to help one another in our duties, yet we are apter far to stir up one another's distempers....

- There is so great a diversity of temperaments and degrees of understanding, that there are scarce any two persons in the world, but there is some unsuitableness between them.... Some crossness there will be of opinion, or disposition, or interest, or will, by nature, or by custom and education, which will stir up frequent discontents....

- And the more they [husband and wife] love each other, the more they participate in each other's griefs....

- And if love make you dear to one another, your parting at death will be the more grievous. And when you first come together, you know that such a parting you must have; through all the course of your lives you may foresee it.[20]

If, having weighed all this, you are still clear that you should marry, choose a God-fearing person of a temperament compatible with your own, lest you "have a domestic war instead of love," advises Baxter. Look for "a competency of wit; for no one can live lovingly and comfortably with a fool," and also for "a power to be silent, as well as to speak; for a babbling tongue is a continual vexation."[21] Richard's feet were always on the ground, and the wisdom of what he says here is obvious.

The mutual duties of husband and wife are listed as love; cohabitation ("a sober and modest conjunction for procreation: avoiding lasciviousness, unseasonableness, and whatever tendeth to corrupt the mind, and make it vain and filthy, and hinder it from holy employment"[22]); fidelity; delight in each other; the practice of quietness and peace ("Agree together beforehand, that when one is in the diseased, angry fit, the other shall silently and gently bear, till it be past and you are come to yourselves again. Be not angry both at once"[23]); spiritual help; care for each other's health and good name; and help in all relevant forms.[24] Elsewhere Richard boils the matter down with beautiful simplicity in question and answer, as follows.

I pray you, next tell me my duty to my wife and hers to me. The common duty of husband and wife is,

1. Entirely to love each other … and avoid all things that tend to quench your love.
2. To dwell together, and enjoy each other, and faithfully join as helpers in the education of their children, the government of the family, and the management of their worldly business.
3. Especially to be helpers of each other's salvation: to stir up each other to faith, love, and obedience, and good works: to warn and help each other against sin, and all temptations; to join in God's worship in the family, and in private: to prepare each other for the approach of death, and comfort each other in the hopes of life eternal.
4. To avoid all dissensions, and to bear with those infirmities in each other which you cannot cure: to assuage, and not provoke, unruly passions; and, in lawful things, to please each other.
5. To keep conjugal chastity and fidelity, and to avoid all unseemly and immodest carriage [conduct] with another, which may stir up jealousy; and yet to avoid all jealousy which is unjust.
6. To help one another to bear their burdens (and not by impatience to make them greater). In poverty, crosses, sickness, dangers, to comfort and support each other. And to be

delightful companions in holy love, and heavenly hopes and duties, when all other outward comforts fail.[25]

Such was the vision for marriage with which Richard and Margaret were armed when they covenanted together to be man and wife. As with so much else in historic Puritanism, one cannot but be struck by the mature, thoughtful, farseeing, fact-facing realism of the whole approach, and feel the contrast with the starry-eyed, shortsighted, self-absorbed goofiness—there really is no other word for it—that marks so many dating and mating couples today. If all spouse-hunting young people were counseled in Baxterian terms regarding marriage, it can safely be said that some of the marriages that happen would never happen, and much of the misery of present-day marriage breakdown would be avoided.

Richard and Margaret themselves, as we shall see, were what we would call "difficult" people, individual to the point of stubbornness, temperamentally at opposite extremes, and with a twenty-year age gap between them; moreover, they were both frequently ill, and were living through a nightmarishly difficult time for persons of their convictions. For Richard, who was officially regarded as the leader and pacesetter of the nonconformists, legal harassment, spying, and personal sniping were constant, making it an invidious thing to be his wife. Yet cheerful patience, fostered by constant mutual encouragement drawn from the Word of God, sustained them throughout, and their relationship prospered and blossomed. Thus was demonstrated not only the grace of God but also the realistic wisdom of the down-to-earth ideal of marriage by which they lived.

To be sure, the Puritans knew all about falling in love. "Marriage love is often a secret work of God," wrote Daniel

Rogers, "pitching the heart of one party upon another for no known cause; and therefore when this strong lodestone attracts each to the other, no further questions need to be made but such a man and such a woman's match were made in heaven, and God has brought them together."[26] But the Puritan emphasis was that, whether or not this delirious "pitching of the heart" is an element in the married couple's present experience, sustained practical friendship and mutual help is in every case a matter of divine command.

So Puritan teachers often said that in choosing a spouse one should look, not necessarily for one whom one *does* love, here and now, in the heart-pitched sense (such a person, if found, might still not be a suitable candidate for a life partnership), but for one whom one *can* love with steady affection on a permanent basis. Once more, Richard brings all this down to earth, stressing that what makes for God-honoring marriage is not euphoria but character, consideration, and commitment: in other words, personal formation, reflection, and resolution.

If God calls you to a married life, expect … trouble … and make particular preparation for each temptation, cross and duty which you must expect. Think not that you are entering into a state of mere [pure and unmixed] delight, lest it prove but a fool's paradise to you. See that you be furnished with marriage strength and patience, for the duties and sufferings of a married state, before you venture on it. Especially, 1. Be well provided against temptations to a worldly mind and life…. 2. See that you be well provided with conjugal affections…. 3. See that you be well provided with marriage prudence and understanding, that you may be able to instruct and edify your families.... [Extended families with servants was the seventeenth-century norm.] 4. See that you be provided with resolvedness and constancy.... Levity and mutability is no fit preparative for a state that only death can change. 5. See that you are well provided with a diligence answerable to the greatness of your undertaken duties.... 6. See that you are well provided with marriage patience; to bear with the infirmities of others, and undergo the daily crosses of your life.... To marry without all this preparation, is as foolish as to go to sea without the necessary preparations for your voyage, or to go to war without armour or ammunition, or to go to work without tools or strength, or to go to buy meat in the market when you have no money.[27]

Marriage preparation today often means no more than suggestions about managing money, handling disagreements, making love, and acting right at the ceremony. Marriage preparation for Richard was a personal spiritual discipline requiring prayerful self-scrutiny in light of all that God wants done and all that may go wrong. The difference is striking and bears a good deal of thinking about. In this as in other matters, modern Christianity is simply not serious and thorough in the Puritan way.

The understanding of marriage involvement in terms of which Richard and Margaret took their vows is now clear. What is not yet clear is how, relationally speaking, they came to their certainty that marriage was right for them. That is what we must look at next.

Love Story

Three fine Baxter scholars of an earlier day[28] found in Richard's memoir—"exquisite," "incomparable," "beautiful," as they describe it[29]—a love story; a story not only of the bereaved husband's love for his wife of almost twenty years, and of their shared love for their God and Savior and for the people they sought to serve, but also of their own heart-pitched love that drew them directly in a unique way to each other. The scholars found this by reading between the lines of Margaret's private papers and Richard's pastoral letters, printed in chapters three and four. Their discernment was, I think, on target, and I suspect it was just what Richard had intended. This is why.

Richard, as N.H. Keeble notes in his ground-breaking study of our author as a literary man, joins in his memoir of Margaret the qualities both of standard Puritan biography, narrating someone's spiritual experience to illustrate universal truths about God's grace to sinners, and of standard modern biography, narrating someone's life experience to highlight that person's three-dimensional individuality. In this, claims Keeble, Richard was "ahead of the taste of his time,"[30] though since he was writing both as Margaret's pastor and as her husband and was aiming to edify specifically members of Margaret's family, who had known her personally, as well as thoughtful readers ("considering men") who had not,[31] he could hardly have written in any other way. But he had a flair for characterizing others and an interest in doing so, which sets him in a class by himself among his Puritan peers.

This interest produced a disagreement of which Richard tells us in some paragraphs of his address "To the Reader" that I edited out.[32] He had wanted to preface the reprint of his funeral sermon for Mary Hanmer, which Margaret's will had mandated, with memoirs not only of Margaret herself but also of three other godly and, to Baxter, dear and admirable people: Mary Hanmer; Mary Baxter, nee Huncks, his own stepmother (whom he confusingly calls his mother-in-law), who had lived in his home for more than a decade and had recently died at age ninety-one; and Jane Matthews, his former housekeeper at Kidderminster, who had died in her mid-seventies a few weeks before. He had actually written these memoirs; but then "wise friends" (unidentified), to whom presumably he showed them, persuaded him that the three additional lives would not be of public interest, and that publishing them would be an error of judgment caused by "love, grief, and nearness.... Affection makes us think our own or our friends' affairs to be such as the world should be affected with: I perceive this weakness and submit."[33] By suppressing and, as it seems, destroying these memoirs he may well have avoided some malicious mockery; but in light of his fascinating skill as a biographer, the loss is ours.

For similar reasons he left out of his memoir of Margaret "the occasions and inducements of our marriage."[34] As he explains:

> The unsuitableness of our age [he forty-seven, she twenty-six: twenty-one years' difference], and my former known purposes against ... the conveniency of ministers' marriage, who have no sort of necessity, made our marriage the matter of much public talk and wonder. And the true opening of her case and mine, and the many strange occurrences which brought it to pass, would take away the wonder of her friends and mine that knew us.... Yet wise friends, by whom I am advised, think it better to omit such personal particularities at least at this time.[35]

Tantalizing! But Richard is not above dropping hints. He does this by the documents he prints in chapters three and four, which deal with the growth of Margaret's soul under his evangelistic instruction and pastoral care. Covering this ground, as he saw it, was the necessary preliminary to his main agenda, namely celebration of the partnership of Margaret and himself through nineteen years of marriage. He put his narrative together, as he tells us, "under the power of melting grief, and therefore perhaps with the less prudent judgment; ... for passionate weakness poureth out all, which greater prudence may conceal";[36] but he kept a firm grip on its structure, and evidently he saw that to deflect satirical sniping and mockery regarding the marriage he must show that the couple were persons totally committed to seek the wisdom, will, and glory of God in their lives. So that is what he does; and the hints are in the documents that he cites for the purpose.

Chapter three begins with the agenda for thanks and petition that Margaret drafted for the prayer warriors' guidance on their day of thanksgiving for her recovery. Then come two private documents "which I saw not till she was dead"[37]—a renewal of her covenant with God and a midnight meditation, both written on the thanksgiving day itself. (To write, as it were, letters of commitment to God and of admonition to oneself was a very Puritan thing to do.) There follows a transcribed letter from Pastor Richard, urging her to share her soul-troubles with her mother and Christian friends, and not to distrust Christ; and two more papers recording Margaret's resolves as the day of thanksgiving approached. The second ended with a resolve "to go to London as soon as I can after the day of thanksgiving."[38] Why? "This following fragment of hers hints something of it [her reason]," writes Richard (he knew!), and he cites a reflection on the fact that means of grace that she once had are hers no longer.[39] Her midnight meditation, written a few days later, was explicit about this, so clearly it was much on her mind:

I have now cause of sorrow for parting with my dear friend, my father, my pastor. He is by Providence called away, and going on a long journey.... I have cause to be humbled that I have been so unprofitable under mercies and means of grace; it may grieve me, now he is gone, that there is so little that came from him left upon my soul.[40]

Plainly her purpose in going to London was to link up with Richard's ministry once more.

In chapter four Richard cites Margaret's transcribings of his own stern admonitions not to let her heart be captured by any "creature," and not to come to London. Then he adds Margaret's closing address to herself, in which she seeks to take to heart what her pastor has told her:

The best creature-affections have a mixture of some creature-imperfections, and therefore need some gall to wean us from the faulty part. God must be known to be God, our rest, and therefore the best creature to be but a creature! O miserable world (how long must I continue in it? and why is this wretched heart so loath to leave it) where we can have no fire without smoke, and our dearest friends must be our greatest grief; and when we begin in hope and love and joy, before we are aware, we fall into an answerable measure of distress. Learn by experience, when any condition is inordinately or excessively sweet to thee, to say, *From hence must be my sorrow*. (O how true!).[41]

What all this shows, as Lloyd-Thomas says, is that "consciously or unconsciously—try as she may to conceal it from him and even from herself—she is already passionately in love with Baxter." He, the brilliant minister whom her masterful mother valued so highly, has become her substitute father (she had long been fatherless) and her dearest friend. It is to him, rather than anyone else, that she wants to talk about her spiritual condition, and from him, rather than anyone else, that she wants to learn the wisdom of God. He is the man in her life, the "creature" who cannot be enjoyed without sorrow, the person whose prospective absence brings grief like a bereavement because already she loves him so much. "But she has no hope of [her love's] earthly fulfilment; he had never given her such encouragement; so far as words of religious counsel could, he has given her every discouragement. She must therefore school herself to break this wild infatuation, and look up to the heavenly life where there are no frustrations, where there is neither marriage nor giving in marriage, but they are as the angels.... What else can she have meant when she wrote in her privacy:

> When the Lord shall take our carcases from the grave, and make us shine as the sun in glory; then, then shall friends meet and never part, and remember their sad and weary nights and days no more! Then may we love freely![42]

Did Richard realize at that time what Margaret was feeling? Almost certainly, yes. Shrewd pastors know what is in the wind, and what may develop, when young women become exclusively dependent on them for spiritual counsel, and they shape their pastoral care accordingly, keeping their distance in order to ensure, so far as they can, that the feelings they discern will not get out of hand. Richard was a shrewd pastor, and that is just what he seems to be doing. He writes Margaret pastoral letters, though she lives only a few yards from the church and from his own lodgings;[43] the letters consistently have a cool, clinical, almost schoolmasterly tone; and they contain explicit warnings against loving any fellow-creature too much.

> How hard it is to keep our hearts from going too far even in honest affections toward the creature, while we are so backward to love God, who should have all the heart and soul and might. Too strong love to any, though it be good in the kind, may be sinful and hurtful in the degree. It will turn too many of your thoughts from God, and they will be too often running after the beloved creature.... It will increase your sufferings by involving you in all the dangers and troubles of those whom you over-love.[44]

> I will pray that no creature may seem greater, better, or more regardable or necessary to you than it is;... that they [creatures] never be over-loved, over-feared, over-trusted, or their thoughts too much regarded.[45]

As Lloyd-Thomas notes, this is hardly the "natural language" of one "who is merely trying to keep the daughter of a parishioner from being over-fondly attached to her mother or too concerned about her brother's attitude."[46] Pastor Richard is clearly trying to redirect what we would call the erotic affection toward himself that Margaret's manner has begun to reveal.

In fact, Richard's interest in this young convert, and his pastoral care for her, had been more than ordinary from the start; partly, no doubt, because of her mother's committed support of his ministry, but partly too, one imagines, because he saw what influence her intelligence, intensity, and social standing would give her in the parish once she was joyfully anchored in Christ. Pastors trying to help people in deep soul-trouble are sometimes obliged to take risks, and Richard took one: he versified her problems and his answers to them and unquestionably gave her copies of the result. This didactic device was, of course, not far from the time-honored practice of wooers writing love poems to their ladies, and must have made Margaret feel she was important to Richard, even if the importance was professedly pastoral and evangelistic rather than amorous and adoring.

The evidence here, which earlier students of our love story seem not to have fully weighed, is in a small book with a large title, *Poetical Fragments: Heart-Imployment* (sic) *with God and Itself. The Concordant Discord of a Broken healed Heart. Sorrowing-rejoycing* (sic), *fearing-hoping, dying-living. Written Partly for himself, and partly for near Friends in Sickness, and other deep Affliction ... Published for the use of the Afflicted.* "The Epistle to the Reader" is dated August 7, 1681, just over two weeks from July 23, the date of the comparable epistle in the memoir, and in it Richard explains why, against the advice of his "wise friends," he is giving this material to the world.

> As they [the poems] were mostly written in various passions, so passion has now thrust them out into the world. God having taken away the dear companion of the last nineteen years of my life, as her sorrows and sufferings long ago gave being to some of these poems (for reasons which the world is not concerned to know) so my grief for her removal, and the revived sense of former things, has prevailed with me to be passionate in the open sight of all.

I confess that passion is often such a hindrance of judgment, that a man should be very suspicious of himself till it be laid [i.e., calmed]: but I am assured that God made it not in vain.... God usually beginneth ... the conversion of sinners, by the awakening of their useful passions, their fear, their grief, repentance, desire, etc.... Lay by all the passionate part of love and joy, and it will be hard to have any pleasant thoughts of heaven....

I will do my wise friends, whose counsel I have much followed, that right [due courtesy] as to acquit them from all the guilt of the publication of these fragments. Some of them say, that *such work is below me*; and those that I think speak wiselier say, *I am below such work*. These I unfeignedly believe.... That I am not excellent, I am satisfied [convinced]. But ... a fiddler may serve at a country wedding....

All that I have to say for these fragments is ... [that their] being suited to afflicted, sick, dying, troubled, sad and doubting persons, the number of such is so great in these calamitous times, as may render them useful to more than I desire.[47]

Some of the poems, writes Baxter, "need an exposition, which I must not give the world"[48] (his wise friends, no doubt, had persuaded him of this), and under these circumstances our conclusions must be tentative. But it looks as if Margaret's "sorrows and sufferings ... gave being" to at least the following:

(7) "Self-Denial. A dialogue between the flesh and the spirit" (240 lines; dated October 29, 1659, when Margaret lay ill).

(8)"The Prayer of the Sick, in a case like Hezekiah's [facing death, praying for life: 2 Kings 20]" (144 lines; undated, but apparently from the same period).

(9)"The Covenant and Confidence of Faith" (64 lines, closing with the statement: "This covenant my dear wife in her former sickness [1659?] subscribed with a cheerful mind").

(12) "The Lamentation for sin afflicting the sinner; especially by the grievous suffering of friends. With the relief of the self-condemning soul" (429 lines, 343 being a dialogue between Jesus and the lamenter, meeting every point in the lament and bringing assurance, or rather reassurance, of his redeeming love and of the lamenter's present and future salvation; dated January 18, 1661, at the beginning and January 26 at the end, the month in which Margaret's much-loved mother was dying).[49]

In that age in which verse was an ordinary gentleman's hobby, one can imagine Pastor Richard showing Margaret these poems and asking her to note that they express and resolve precisely her own inner conflicts and uncertainties, pointing out to her the path of peace—as indeed they do. To show this in detail is not possible here, but I reprint two of these poems at the end of the memoir (page 151) so that readers may match them with what chapters three and four show of Margaret's inner turmoil in 1659-60 and draw their own conclusions.[50]

This is how the matter appears to me: Margaret had sought conversion in the sense in which Richard's 1657 sermons had described it:[51] that is, as a regenerating work of God the Holy Spirit imparting to mind, heart, and life a new, humble, prayerful, radically God-centered and Christ-focused orientation, thus reversing the natural godlessness of our fallen existence. As an unconverted life is under God's judicial sentence of death and hell, so conversion conveys divine promises of pardon, peace, and protection. Margaret's quest for conversion, pursued by self-examination, self-humbling, prayerful penitence, and attempts at a sincere and wholehearted covenanting commitment to Christ, led, probably early in 1659, to a sense of assurance whereby she found herself convinced that God had pardoned and accepted her, that she was indeed a new creature in Christ, and that she had been instated as an heir of heaven's glory.

This was the usual, and surely scriptural, form of Puritan conversion. But for some time after assurance dawned, anything untoward—illness, disappointment, trouble coming to those she loved and had prayed for, or whatever—threw her into turmoil lest, after all, she was a self-deceived hypocrite and the untoward event was God telling her so. So she needed constant help to humble herself afresh, renew her covenant with God in Christ, strengthen her grip on God's promises, grasp more firmly that trouble is part of the divine plan for our lives, and get back to praising and hoping as habits of the heart to be maintained through thick and thin. Richard's letters and poems, and the one-on-one admonitions that undoubtedly accompanied them e all designed to give her self-understanding and help at this point. The Lord blessed, and by the time of their marriage the lessons had been well learned.

Meanwhile, a final question: Did Richard intend his readers to pick up all these hints I have highlighted about Margaret's feelings for him and his ministry to her as to someone special during 1659-60, when he was still wholeheartedly committed to clerical bachelorhood? The best guess is that he did not care one way or the other. For him the important thing was to share what might help others; that purpose was both his guiding star and the boundary of his concern. We honor his and Margaret's memory best by keeping that purpose in view as now we proceed.

Mr. and Mrs. Baxter

The marriage of Richard and Margaret was a very happy one. "When we were married, her sadness and melancholy vanished: counsel did something to it, and contentment something; and being taken up with our household affairs did somewhat. And we lived in inviolated love and mutual complacency sensible of the benefit of mutual help. These near nineteen years I know not that we had any breach in the point of love, or point of interest, save only that she somewhat grudged that I had persuaded her for my quietness to surrender so much of her estate, as disabled her from helping others so much as she earnestly desired."[52]

It might have seemed that the odds were against such happiness. There was a twenty-one-year age gap between them; Margaret, a convert of three years or so, was marrying a veteran clergyman who had been ordained when she was only two years old; and they were both of fragile health, though in different ways, Margaret being a martyr to migraines and chest congestion and Richard being a veritable museum of diseases, which meant that he lived in some degree of pain most of the time. He was forthright and hasty, and could be strident; she was gentle and circumspect, and could not bear an angry voice. Also, they were differently conditioned by their social backgrounds, with consequences that might easily have been explosive. "I had been bred among plain, lower-class people, and I thought that so much washing of stairs and rooms, to keep them as clean as their trenchers and dishes, and so much ado about cleanliness and trifles, was a sinful eccentricity and expense of servants' time, who might that while have been reading some good book. But she that was otherwise bred had somewhat other thoughts."[53]

There was more. They had to move house several times, and wherever Richard was and whatever he was doing he was the object of continual spying and sniping; he was the tall poppy among Puritan nonconformists, and devotees of restored Anglicanism were determined to find ways of cutting him down. Then, too, Richard was a public man, a preacher and a tireless writer, constantly in the home but not available to Margaret. It cannot have been easy for her, even though, as was usual with aristocratic ladies, she had in their home for much of the time a companion of her own sex.

Moreover, neither of them had a really easy temperament. Margaret was highly strung and a bundle of fears inside, which she made worse by bottling them up; Richard was hasty and frequently offhand, as persons who live in pain often are, and was inclined to be downcast and irritable when things did not go his way. He is talking from experience when he declares: "The pleasing of a wife is usually no easy task. There is an unsuitableness in the best and wisest and most alike. Faces are not so unlike as the apprehensions of the mind. They that agree in religion, in love and interest, yet may have different apprehensions about occasional occurrences, persons, things, words, etc. That will seem the best way to one that seems the worst to the other. And passions are apt to succeed and serve these differences. Very good people are hard to be pleased. My own dear wife had high desires of my doing and speaking better than I did, but my badness made it hard for me to do better."[54] Again: "My dear wife did look for more good in me than she found, especially lately in my weakness and decay. We are all like pictures that must not be looked on too near. They that come near us find more faults and badness in us than others at a distance know."[55] Yet, despite their real limitations of temperament and character, they achieved a marvelously happy and fruitful partnership.

Richard's admiration for Margaret was unbounded. She was "a woman of extraordinary acuteness of wit, solidity and judgment, incredible prudence and sagacity and sincere devotedness to God, and unusual strict obedience to him ... who ... heaped on me ... many and great obligations to love and tenderness."[56] "She was very desirous that we should all have lived in a constancy of devotion and a blameless innocency. And in this respect she was the meetest helper that I could have had in the world;... for I was apt to be over-careless in my speech and too backward to my duty, and she was always endeavoring to bring me to greater wariness and strictness in both. If I spoke rashly or sharply, it offended her; if I behaved (as I was apt) with too much neglect of ceremony or humble compliment to any, she would modestly tell me of it; if my very looks seemed not pleasant, she would have me amend them (which my weak pained state of body undisposed me to do); if I forgot any week to catechize my servants and familiarly instruct them personally (besides my ordinary family duties [i.e., household prayers twice daily]), she was troubled at my remissness."[57] He did not think her flawless, just a wonderful partner; and no doubt she had similar thoughts to the end of her days about him.

Many things, of course, were going for them. They were one in faith, in hope of glory, in their approach to the tasks of marriage, and in their commitment to a rejoicing lifestyle. "After all the doubts of her sincerity and salvation and all the fears and sadness thereupon, which cast her into melancholy,[58] she so far overcame them all, that for near these nineteen years that I have lived with her, I think I never heard her thrice speak a doubting word of her salvation, but oft of her hopeful persuasions that we should live together in heaven; it being my judgment and constant practice to make those that I teach understand that the gospel is glad tidings of great joy; and that holiness lies especially in delighting in God, his Word and works, and in his joyful praise and hopes of glory, and in longing for and seeking the heavenly Jerusalem, and in living as fruitfully to the church and others as we can do in the world; and that this must be wrought by the most believing apprehensions of God's goodness as equal to his greatness, and of his great love to mankind manifested in our redemption, and by believing the grace and riches of Christ and the comforting office of the Holy Ghost, and studying daily God's promises and mercies and our everlasting joys; and that religion consists in doing God's commanding will and quietly and joyfully trusting in his promising and disposing will; and that fear and sorrow are but to remove impediments and further all this.

"And this doctrine by degrees she drunk in and so fully consented to that (though timorousness was her disease) her judgment was quieted and settled therein."[59]

They sang together. "It was not the least comfort that I had in the converse of my late dear wife, that our first in the morning, and last in bed at night was a psalm of praise."[60] Though they discovered over and over again that marriage brings trouble, shared joy was the dominant tone of their relationship throughout.

Though wise, winning, patient, self-possessed, brave, and generous to a fault, Margaret had her vulnerabilities. For her constant scheming to enable her husband to preach while others schemed to silence him, and for the many charitable initiatives she took as she went along, she can hardly be overpraised; yet she could be obsessive and overoptimistic about her projects, and then prostrated with disappointment when things did not turn out as she had hoped. She could be "righteous overmuch," in the sense of concentrating so intensely on one duty that she would forget other, greater duties. She was culpably slow to talk to others about spiritual matters. "I scarce ever met with a person that was abler to speak long, for matter and good language, even about religious things," writes Richard; "... and yet she could not do it herself for fear of seeming to be guilty of ostentation. In good company she would speak little of that which she most desired to hear. When I was at any time from home, she would not pray in the family.... Most of the open speaking part of religion she omitted, through a diseased enmity to ostentation and hypocrisy."[61]

She was obsessive about her health, too, spending much of her adult life in fear of mental collapse,[62] starving herself for years for fear that overeating would bring on cancer,[63] and thereby as it seems undermining her own constitution. "Her understanding," writes Richard, "... was higher and clearer than other people's, but, like the treble strings of a lute, strained up to the highest, sweet, but in continual danger."[64] She "proved her sincerity by her costliest obedience. It cost her ... somewhat of her trouble of body and mind; for her knife was too keen and cut the sheath. Her desires were more earnestly set on doing good than her tender mind and head could well bear."[65]

But she gave Richard magnificent support all along the line. Though, as she told him, she wished he would write less and do it more carefully,[66] she never complained at the endless hours he spent pen-pushing; nor at the wretched circumstances of their life during the hard winter of 1669-70, when "the coal smoke so filled the room that we were all day sat in that it was as a cloud, and we were even suffocated with the stink. And she had ever a great constriction of the lungs that could not bear smoke or closeness."[67] On the occasion when Baxter's home preaching landed him in Clerkenwell jail with a six-month sentence, she "cheerfully went with me into prison; she brought her best bed thither.... I think she scarce ever had a pleasanter time in her life."[68] "This history (and my great experience)," he writes, "saith that *there is a friend that sticketh closer than a brother*, Proverbs 18:24."[69] From his story one sees entirely what he means.

As for Richard himself, it is clear that the blend of theological sternness, pastoral tenderness, husbandly humility and personal realism in his memoir reflects the way his life with Margaret was actually lived. In writing the memoir he has nothing to prove and nothing to hide, since he does not think he is long for this world. There is poignant dignity in his closing paragraph:

> In our greatest straits and sufferings, let us comfort one another with these words: *That we shall for ever be with the Lord.* Had I been to possess the company of my friends in this life only, how short would our comfortable converse have been! But now I shall live with them in the heavenly city of God for ever. And they, being there of the same mind with my forgiving God and Savior, will forgive all my failings, neglects, and injuries, as God forgiveth them and me. The Lord gave, and the Lord hath taken away; and he hath taken away but that upon my desert, which he had given me undeservedly near nineteen years.... I am waiting to be next. The door is open. Death will quickly draw the veil and make us see how near we were to God and one another, and did not

sufficiently know it. Farewell vain world, and welcome true everlasting life.[70]

"We meet two exceptional and exemplary Christians in this book," writes N.H. Keeble; "we also meet, as we rarely do in seventeenth-century biographies, two very human characters."[71] That is true, and that is why we resonate so deeply with Richard as he celebrates his nineteen years of great gladness with a great Puritan lady. It is now time to let him tell us the story in his own words.

Part Two

Great Goodness:
Richard on Margaret
(The Breviate)

Editor's Note

RICHARD BAXTER WAS A COMMUNICATIVE MAN, THE KIND OF MAGNETIC, COMMANDING PERSON WHO MAKES YOU FEEL THAT HE IS TAKING YOU INTO HIS CONFIDENCE EVERY TIME HE OPENS HIS MOUTH OR PUTS PEN TO PAPER. AUGUSTINE, LUTHER, C.S. LEWIS, AND BILLY GRAHAM ARE FOUR MORE INSTANCES OF THIS HUMAN TYPE—ALL OF THEM, INCIDENTALLY, PERSONS WITH WHOM IN DIFFERENT WAYS BAXTER IS COMPARABLE.

IT IS CLEAR THAT RICHARD WROTE VERY MUCH AS HE TALKED, BOTH IN ORDINARY CONVERSATION AND IN THE PULPIT; AND THE WAY SHREWD PRECISION COMBINES WITH GUILELESS SPONTANEITY IN ALL HIS BOOKS GIVES THEM A FLAVOR OF MAGISTERIAL PATHOS THAT IS UNIQUE, AND QUITE RIVETING. THE BAXTER WRITING STYLE IS LOOSE BUT LUCID; IT IS INTIMATE, INFORMAL, REPETITIVE, AND SCHOOLMASTERLY, YET ALWAYS POINTED AND WEIGHTY, COMING HOT FROM BOTH HEAD AND HEART. RICHARD'S POWERS OF ANALYSIS AND ARTICULATION ENSURED THAT ALL HIS WRITING IS CLEAR AND STRONG, EVEN WHEN EXACT GRAMMAR FAILS; AND HIS ZEAL FOR GOD'S GLORY, THE CHURCH'S PURITY, AND THE HEALTH OF SOULS MADE IT CONSTANTLY ARDENT AND ARRESTING.

SOMEONE COINED THE PHRASE "NOBLE NEGLIGENCE" TO DESCRIBE RICHARD'S WAY OF WRITING; IT FITS PERFECTLY. SURE THAT HIS TIME WAS SHORT AND THAT THERE WAS A VAST AMOUNT OF WORK STILL WAITING FOR HIM TO DO, HE WROTE AT TOP SPEED AND PUBLISHED WITH LITTLE OR NO REVISION, SO THAT EVERYTHING IS BRISK, FRANK, ROUGH, AND PUNGENT, THE LITERARY LEGACY OF A GOOD MAN IN A HURRY. THE SUBJECT MATTER OF THE BREVIATE, AND THE OVERTONES OF GRIEF THAT MARK ITS PAGES, SET IT APART FROM THE REST OF BAXTER'S BOOKS, BUT IT IS VINTAGE BAXTER IN RESPECT OF ALL THE QUALITIES MENTIONED SO FAR.

RICHARD OFFERS THE BOOK AS TRUE AND USEFUL HISTORY—USEFUL, THAT IS, IN THE SENSE THAT IT ILLUSTRATES PRINCIPLES ABOUT LIFE WITH AND UNDER GOD THAT WILL GUIDE AND ENCOURAGE CHRISTIAN READERS. MORE THAN ONCE RICHARD ANTICIPATES THE CRITICISM THAT THE

BREVIATE IS A SELF-PITYING OR SELF-APPLAUDING EGO TRIP BY INSISTING ON ITS USEFULNESS, AND HE TITLES ITS LAST CHAPTER, ALMOST DEFIANTLY, "SOME USES PROPOSED TO THE READER FROM THIS HISTORY, AS THE REASONS WHY I WROTE IT" ("USES" MEANS HERE "APPLICATORY LESSONS").

THIS WAS A VERY PURITAN CONCERN ON BAXTER'S PART. IN ALL THEIR COMMUNICATIONS AND COMMITMENTS, THE PURITANS SOUGHT TO OBSERVE A MAXIM THAT MIGHT BE CALLED THE PRINCIPLE OF PARSIMONY, NAMELY THAT THERE IS NO PLACE IN LIFE FOR IDLE WORDS OR AIMLESS ACTIONS, BUT THAT EVERYTHING SAID AND DONE SHOULD COUNT FOR THE CAUSE OF GOD AND THE GOOD OF HIS PEOPLE. WHETHER OR NOT PURITANS AS A BODY PUSHED THIS PRINCIPLE SO FAR AS TO CONSTRICT CHRISTIAN LIBERTY IS DEBATABLE, BUT THERE CAN BE NO DEBATE THAT THE PRINCIPLE ITSELF IS TRUE, AND BASIC TO RESPONSIBLE CHRISTIAN LIVING. WE MAY WELL BE GLAD THAT BAXTER WAS CONCERNED TO OBSERVE IT, FOR HIS CHAIN OF "USES" (TWENTY-ONE, ALL TOLD) OFFERS INSIGHTS ON CHRISTIAN LIFE AND MARRIAGE THAT ARE GOLDEN IN QUALITY. "THEY AMOUNT TO THE CONTENTION THAT HIS WIFE'S EXPERIENCES CAN ENCOURAGE HOPE, DISCOURAGE DESPAIR, AND PREVENT FALSE EXPECTATIONS BY SHOWING WHAT A SAINT MAY EXPECT IN THIS WORLD, AND THAT HER EXAMPLE MAY GUIDE OTHERS."[1]

HONESTY, HUMILITY, AND THE WORLD-WEARINESS BROUGHT ON BY HIS OWN WEAKNESS OF BODY AND GRIEF OF MIND COMBINE TO GIVE GREAT AUTHORITY, AS WELL AS GREAT POIGNANCY, TO THE LESSONS FROM MARGARET'S STORY THAT THE BEREAVED PASTOR-TEACHER DRAWS OUT.

MY GOAL IN EDITING THE BREVIATE HAS BEEN TO LET BAXTER SPEAK TO MODERN READERS AS STRAIGHTFORWARDLY AS POSSIBLE. SO I HAVE CUT OUT A FEW PARAGRAPHS THAT CLUTTER UP THE STORY, MODERNIZED SPELLING AND PUNCTUATION, EXPLAINED ARCHAISMS IN BRACKETS, AND ADDED OR SUBSTITUTED A FEW WORDS TO SECURE A SMOOTHER FLOW. SINCE RICHARD THOUGHT OF HIMSELF AS WRITING FOR POSTERITY NO LESS THAN FOR HIS CONTEMPORARIES, I DO NOT THINK HE WOULD OBJECT TO WHAT I HAVE DONE. THE EDITION OF THE BREVIATE FOR

SCHOLARS REMAINS J.T. WILKINSON'S SUPERB *RICHARD BAXTER AND MARGARET CHARLTON: A PURITAN LOVE-STORY* (1928), SADLY LONG OUT OF PRINT. I GRATEFULLY ACKNOWLEDGE THE HELP THAT WILKINSON'S WORK HAS BEEN IN MY OWN ENTERPRISE. THE PHOTOGRAPHS ON PAGES 16 AND 17 ARE OF PORTRAITS THAT WILKINSON REPRODUCED.

To the Reader

Reader,

God having called away to his blessed rest and glory the spirit of the most dear companion of these last nineteen years of my life, or near; I found in her last will a request that I should reprint five hundred of her mother's funeral sermons, written by me in 1661, being now out of print, called *The Last Work of a Believer, His Passing Prayer, etc.* Not only her very great love and honor of her remembered mother moved her to it, but the apprehension of the usefulness of that subject to dying Christians; a subject about which her soul was awakened the more by the death of many friends and excellent Christians taken away this year. And the day somewhat excited her, for the will was written by her on December 30, 1680, the same day which she kept secretly as an anniversary remembrance of the sentence of death from which she had been delivered;[2] and the same day when our dear friend, Mr. Corbet, lay dying. And I find some expectations of her own speedy death had some hand in it.

Being thus obliged by her request, mine own affections urged me to prefix this *Breviate* of her own life, written, I confess, under the power of melting grief, and therefore perhaps with the less prudent judgment; but not with the less, but the more truth; for passionate weakness poureth out all, which greater prudence may conceal. Conscientious men's histories are true; but if they be also wise, they tell us but some part of the truth, concealing that which would do harm and which the depraved world cannot bear without abusing it. But we that are less wise tell all the truth, too little regarding how men will receive it.

That which is left out of the narrative of my wife's life is the occasions and inducements of our marriage and some passages between some relatives and her, which the world is not concerned (yet at least) to know.[3]

If this that is written seem useless to any, it will not hurt them, if they leave it to others that find it more suitable to them: All things be not agreeable to all. That may be useful to persons of her own quality, which is not so to many others. To her nephews and nieces and some other kindred, who were also near to her and for whose sake above most others I write it, you cannot think it will be altogether useless. O that they would imitate her in all that is praiseworthy and needful to themselves. The grand objection I foresee will be that I seem to parade some of mine own good works by praising hers.[4] And must I needs bury the memory of them as hers, for fear of the sting of such objectors? I have told them truly it is not my own acts, but those that were properly hers that I there mention. It is not her giving of my money which I there recite, but that which either was her own and none of mine, or else procured by her for those uses; and the works were of a kind, in which I was but the executor of her will.

She is gone after many of my choicest friends, who within this one year are gone to Christ, and I am following even at the door. Had I been to enjoy them only here, it would have been but a short comfort, mixed with the many troubles which all our failings and sins, and some degree of unsuitableness between the nearest and dearest, cause. But I am going after them to that blessed society where life, light, and love, and therefore harmony, concord, and joy, are perfect and everlasting.

Reader, while I give thee but the truth, forgive the effects of age, weakness, and grief. The Lord prosper our preparation for our great approaching change. To leave this world for ever and enter upon an endless life, where we shall speed according to the preparations of this little inch of time, doth certainly bespeak the most serious thoughts, the wisest and speediest care and diligence, the most patient suffering, the most unwearied labor, the most frugal use of all our time, the most resolute resistance to all temptations, and to the faithful, the most joyful hopes.

RICH. BAXTER
July 23, 1681

One

Of Her Parentage and the Occasion of Our Acquaintance

[MARGARET'S WIDOWED MOTHER MOVES TO KIDDERMINSTER, WHERE RICHARD IS THE PASTOR, AND EXERCISES A POTENT CHRISTIAN INFLUENCE THERE. MARGARET JOINS HER.]

AS I KNEW MORE OF THIS PERSON than any other, for the good of the readers and the honor of God's grace in her, I shall by God's assistance truly report the things which I know.

We were born in the same county within three miles and an half of each other; but she of one of the chief families in the county, and I but of a mean low-grade freeholder (called a gentleman for his ancestors' sake, but of a small estate, though sufficient). Her father, Francis Charlton, Esq., was one of the best justices of the peace in that county, a grave and sober worthy man, but he did not marry till he was aged and gray, and so died while his children were very young, who were three, of which the eldest daughter and his only son are yet alive.

[BAXTER NOW TELLS IN DETAIL HOW MARGARET'S WIDOWED MOTHER BECAME MRS. HANMER BY REMARRIAGE, HOW DURING THE CIVIL WAR HER HOME WAS BURNED, AND HOW AGAINST BAXTER'S ADVICE SHE SUBSEQUENTLY MOVED TO KIDDERMINSTER IN ORDER TO BENEFIT FROM HIS MINISTRY.]

When she had been there alone a while, her unmarried daughter, Margaret (about seventeen or eighteen years of age), came after her from her brother's, resolving not to forsake the mother who deserved her dearest love; and sometime went to Oxford to her elder sister (wife to Mr. Ambrose Upton, then Canon of Christ's Church, both yet living). In this time the good old mother lived as a blessing amongst the honest poor weavers of Kidderminster, strangers to her, whose company for their piety she chose before all the vanities of the world. In which time my acquaintance with her made me know, that (notwithstanding she had formerly been somewhat passionate [i.e., prone to violent gusts of emotion, especially anger, and mood swings]) she was a woman of all that manly patience in her great trials, that prudence and piety, and justice and impartiality and other virtues which I mentioned in her funeral sermon. Of her death anon. It is her daughter's case that this is the prologue to.

Two

Of Her Conversion, Sickness, and Recovery

[MARGARET BECOMES FIRST A SEEKER, AND THEN A FINDER,
OF NEW LIFE IN CHRIST. RICHARD QUOTES A WRITTEN REAC-
TION TO ONE OF HIS SERMONS, IN WHICH SHE JUDGES HER-
SELF TO BE CHRISTLESS. SOON AFTER HER CONVERSION SHE IS
HEALED OF A LIFE-THREATENING ILLNESS THROUGH SPECIAL
PRAYER WITH FASTING ON HER BEHALF BY A GROUP OF PRAYER
WARRIORS IN THE PARISH, INCLUDING RICHARD HIMSELF.]

IN HER VAIN YOUTH, pride and romances, and company suitable
thereto, did take her up; and an imprudent *rigid* governess that
her mother had set over her in her absence had done her hurt, by
possessing her with ill thoughts of strictness in religion; yet she had
a great reverence for some good ministers (especially Mr. Thos.
Wright),⁵ and she thought that she was not what she should be,
but something better (she knew not what) must be attained. In
this case coming to Kidderminster for mere love to her mother,
she had great aversion to the poverty and strictness of the people
there, glittering herself in costly apparel and delighting in her
romances. But in a little time she heard and understood what
those better things were which she had thought must be attained.

And a sermon of Mr. H. Hickman's⁶ at Oxford much moved
her (on Isaiah 27:11: *It is a people of no understanding, therefore he
that made them will not save them,* etc.). The doctrine of conversion (as I preached it as now in my treatise of conversion)⁷ was
received on her heart as the seal on the wax. Whereupon she

presently fell to self-judging, and to frequent prayer, and to reading and serious thoughts on her present state and her salvation.

A religious maid that waited on her, taking notice of this (for she kept all her matters so secret to herself, as was her great hurt all her life), acquainted her mother with it; and when it would be hid no longer, but her frequent closet-prayers were sometimes overheard, and her changed course of life discerned, her mother (who, as far as I could discern, previously loved her least of her three children) began to esteem her as her darling; and all her religious friends and neighbors were glad of so sudden and great a change.

I will here give you one of her self-judging papers which I find since her death, upon her then sad convictions. When I had on Romans 8:9 told them how it may be known whether we have Christ's Spirit or not, she thus repeated the signs with her self-condemnation.

> Mark 1.—*The Spirit of Christ is the Author of the Scriptures and therefore suiteth your disposition to it, and guideth you by it.*
>> Judgm. 1.—I fear then I have not the Spirit of Christ; for I yet feel no love to God's Word, nor closure with it as suitable to me, but I am questioning the truth of it, or at best quarreling with it.
>
> Mark 2.—*The Spirit of Christ is from heaven, from God our Father, and leadeth us upward unto him. Its work is spiritual, of heavenly tendency, making us cry Abba! Father! and working the heart by uniting love to God.*
>> Judgm. 2.—It is not so with me; for I have a spirit tending only to selfishness and sin.
>
> Mark 3.—*The Spirit of Christ uniteth us to Christ and one another by love and is against hatred, division, and abusing others.*
>> Judgm. 3—Mine then is the spirit of Cain, for I cannot

endure any that are not of my opinion and way, and it inclineth me to malice and unpeaceableness and division.

Mark 4.—*The Spirit of Christ is a Spirit of holiness and doth not favor licentiousness in doctrine or in life.*

Judgm. 4.—Though I am for strict principles, I am loose in practice.

Mark 5.—*Christ's Spirit inclineth to love, humility, and meekness, and makes men stoop to each other for their good.*

Judgm. 5—None more uncharitable, proud, and censorious than I.

Mark 6.—*The Spirit of Christ makes men little, low, and vile in their own eyes; it is pride that puffeth up.*

Judgm. 6.—My self-conceitedness shows that I am unhumbled.

Mark 7.—*The Spirit of Christ doth work to the mortifying of the flesh, even all its inordinate desires, and to self-denial.*

Judgm. 7.—I am a stranger to the work of mortification and self-denial. I can deny myself nothing but the comfort of well-doing. I cannot deny my sloth so far as to go to prayer when I am convinced of my necessity.

Mark 8.—*The Spirit of Christ is a prevailing Spirit, and doth not only wish and strive, but overcome the flesh as to its rule.*

Judgm. 8.—The flesh prevaileth with me against the Spirit.

Mark 9.—*Christ's Spirit is the author of his worship and ordinances, and suits the souls of believers to them, the Word, sacraments, etc.*

Judgm. 9.—They seem not suitable to my soul; I am against them, and had rather not use them, if I dared neglect them.

Mark 10.—*Christ's Spirit is in all the saints, and inclineth them to holy communion with each other in love, especially with those in whom this Spirit most eminently worketh.*

> Judgm. 10.—It is not thus with me: I desire not the communion of saints; my affections are most to those who are best to me, whether they have more or less of the Spirit.

To go no further, it is now evident that I am a graceless person. Though all these things be imperfect in the best, and some are more wanting in one particular than another; yet where all their contraries are predominant, as in me, that person is told by this sermon that they are none of Christ's; how much doth my behavior at this time make this appear, when I can with a hard heart and a dry eye and a steady hand declare myself at present heir of everlasting woe! But the longest day will quickly come, though I strive to put it as far from me.

It would be too long to recite a paper which I find next to this, containing the great necessity of self-judging, the reason for it, the rules of performing it, and the due manner; especially in dangers, and before the sacraments, or any conclusions about our state of grace.

But these convictions did neither die, nor yet pass unto despair, but to serious conversion; yet put her to struggle hard against aversion to secret duties, and to the forsaking of some vanities; but presently God seemed suddenly to welcome this returning soul. And while we were all rejoicing in her change, she fell into a cough and seeming consumption [a wasting disease, such as tuberculosis], in which we almost despaired of her life. Mr. Jackson, the physician, and myself, seeing the case too hard for us, described it to Dr. Prujean and Dr. G. Bates, who both judged it a consumption arising from the obstructions of the vessels in the lungs and corrupting the tender adjoining parts, and both prescribed her the same medicines.[8] But all these, and the change of air long [i.e., over a period of time],[9] and breast-milk, etc., did no good. I and my praying neighbors were so sorry that such a changed person should presently be taken away before she had time to manifest her sincerity and do God any service in the world, that in grief they resolved to fast and pray for her. For former experience had lately much raised their belief in the success of prayer. They had lately prayed for one that seemed demoniac that (after some years' misery) was suddenly freed of that disease. They had often prayed for me in dangerous illness, and I had speedy help. I had lately swallowed a gold-bullet for a medicine,[10] and it lodged in me long, and no means would bring it away, till they met to fast and pray, and it came away that morning. A young man, yet living, falling into a violent epilepsy, and after all means long remaining uncured, they set to fasting and praying in his hearing, and the second day he was suddenly cured, and never had a fit since. God did not deny their prayers, though they were *without book* [i.e., not taken from the Anglican Book of Common Prayer, or any similar source], and such as some deride as extempore. I was not with them in any of these, but laymen that were humble praying persons only.

But I was with them at prayer for this woman; and compassion made us all extraordinary fervent, and God heard us and speedily delivered her as it were by nothing or by an altogether undesigned means. She drank of her own inclination, not being directed, a large quantity of syrup of violets, and the next morning her nose bled (which scarce ever did before or since) and the lungs seemed cleared, and her pulse suddenly amended, her cough abated, and her strength returned in a short time.

Three

Of the Workings of Her Soul in and after This Sickness

[RICHARD FIRST PRESENTS THREE DOCUMENTS THAT MARGARET WROTE IN CONNECTION WITH THE DAY OF THANKSGIVING FOR HER RECOVERY THAT HER MOTHER ORGANIZED. A PERSONAL STATEMENT OF MATTERS FOR THANKSGIVING AND PRAYER, WHICH SHE OFFERED AS AN AGENDA TO THE PRAYER WARRIORS, IS FOLLOWED BY TWO PRIVATE OUTPOURINGS ON PAPER, ONE A RENEWAL OF HER PERSONAL COVENANT WITH GOD AND ONE A LONG, RUTHLESSLY HONEST, SELF-CENSURING, AND SELF-ENCOURAGING ACCOUNT OF HER RESTLESS SPIRITUAL STATE, FINISHED AND SIGNED AT MIDNIGHT ON THE THANKSGIVING DAY. RICHARD THEN PRINTS A PASTORAL LETTER FROM HIMSELF, CHIDING HER FOR YIELDING TO FEAR AND UNBELIEF AND NOT BEING MORE OPEN ABOUT HER SPIRITUAL STRUGGLES, AND ADDS TO THIS THREE MORE WRITTEN MESSAGES FROM HERSELF TO HERSELF EXPRESSING DIFFERENT FACETS OF HER RESOLVE TO CLEAVE TO GOD FULLY.]

SINCE SHE WAS OF TOO TIMOROUS AND TENDER A NATURE, and the sharp work of her repentance was yet upon her spirit: for death to come and seem to summon her away to eternity at such a season and in such an unsettled state, must needs greatly increase her fears, when the strongest long-experienced Christians find it no easy work to die in peace, and willing resignation. But she had always a concealing temper, which made it never the easier within.

When God had recovered her, her mother invited those that fasted and prayed for her to keep a day of thanksgiving for her deliverance. I asked her what she would have us give thanks for particularly? And in the morning as we began, she (that was recovered) gave us this following paper:

My life hath been a life of very great mercies, and these have aggravated my sin in overlooking them. Some of those which God hath most affected my heart with, I shall here mention; but alas! with a heart very insensible to the greatness of them.

My mother's restoration first I thank God for; and next for many mercies of mine own. Four times before this I have been delivered from great danger of death.[11]

And now I desire to acknowledge his mercy in delivering me from this death-threatening disease, and that in answer to prayers I am here now in competent health to speak of the goodness of the Lord.

I desire to acknowledge it a mercy that God should afflict me; and though I cannot with the Psalmist say, *But now I keep thy statutes;* I can say, *Before I was afflicted I went astray.* And how many great sins God hath prevented by this affliction, I cannot tell; but I am sure that God hath dealt very graciously with me; and I have had many comforts in my sufferings, which God hath not given to many of his beloved ones.

I desire to acknowledge God's great mercy to me in bringing me to this town, under so useful means of grace; and that at such time when I was ready to engage in a course of sin and vanity beyond what I had formerly lived in. This mercy is made much greater by the time; for had the Lord brought me hither in infancy and removed me at riper years, the mercy would not have been so great. And if I had gone longer on in a course of hardening sins, it had been less than now it is.

I desire to acknowledge it a great mercy that I want no outward thing, but am enabled to be helpful unto others and have all the temporal mercies I can well desire for my encouragement in the ways of God.

I desire to acknowledge it a great mercy that God hath given me an interest in the hearts and prayers of so many of his faithful servants in this place.

I desire to acknowledge it a great mercy that God hath made me the child of godly parents, and a child of many prayers.

I desire to acknowledge it a great mercy, which I can never be thankful enough for, that God hath given me a heart in any measure willing to acknowledge his mercies and be thankful for them; and that notwithstanding all that sin and Satan hath done to hinder it, he hath made me desirous this day to give up myself and all that I have to him, taking him only for my God and my chief felicity.

And now the requests that I desire you to make on my behalf are these:

That he will give me a more thankful soul, that I may praise him all my days.

And an humble heart, that I may be taught of God, who looketh on the proud afar off.

And a tender conscience, that I may fear to offend him and hate all sin.

And strength so to resist temptations, that I be not led by Satan to dishonor God or to provoke him.

And a meek and quiet frame of spirit, that I may be contented to bear the afflictions that God shall lay me under without murmuring or repining.

This being that which she gave us, I find under her hand this secret renewal that same day of her covenant with God, which I annex.

This being a day set apart for returning thanks to God for his mercy in delivering me from the gates of death, these people being they that have earnestly supplicated the throne of grace on my behalf, I here now renew my covenant with almighty God and resolve by his grace to endeavor to get and keep a fresh sense of his mercy on my soul, and a greater sense yet of my sin; I resolve to set myself against my sin with all my might, and not to take its part or extenuate it or keep the devil's counsel, as I have done, to the wronging of God and the wounding of my own soul. I resolve by God's assistance to set upon the practice of known duty, and not to study shifts and evasions to put off those duties which are either troublesome, chargeable [i.e., costing money], or likely to render me dishonorable and vile in the eyes of the carnal persons of the world. And this I do upon these considerations and for these reasons.

My life hath been a life of great mercy. God hath preserved it more than this once and hath done exceeding great things for me, which engageth me more than many others, though all rational creatures are obliged to live to God their Maker.

God hath not only given me life, but in some measure ability and opportunity to do him service; yea, and already some encouragement in the hopes of the success of some of my poor endeavors. (I suppose on some of her servants.)[12]

God hath more engaged me to himself by taking me into

his family and planting me in his garden and watering me with the dew from heaven. He hath set me in a fruitful soil; he hath given me the high privilege of a part in the hearts and prayers of his people; and I may say that I live to speak it, that God is a God who hears prayers, and hath heard and answered them. Though the tempter be busy to make me think diminutively of this great mercy, yet I must not, but must acknowledge the greatness of it.

As all these and more engagements are upon me, so I am already engaged by the baptismal covenant to God the Father, Son, and Holy Ghost; and to the Father as my God and chief good and only happiness; and to the Son as my Redeemer, Head, and Husband; and to the Holy Ghost as my Sanctifier and Comforter; and I have renewed it in the sacrament of the Lord's Supper; and how can I go back that have thus far engaged myself and daily receive from God more obligations? Yea, God will expect more from me than from many others. Let me therefore see that I be in good earnest with God and think not to put him off with hypocrisy. Let me not deceive myself, for God will not be mocked; what I sow, I shall reap. If I belong to God, though I suffer whilst I am in the body, they will be but light afflictions and but for a moment; but the everlasting Kingdom will be mine inheritance. And when this life is ended, I shall reign with Christ; I shall be freed from sin and suffering and for ever rejoice with saints and angels. But should I prove a hypocrite, I lose my labor, I lose my God; and damnation with devils and damned ones will be my reward for ever, and this the greater as my mercies have been abundant and great.

Therefore I here desire this day to renew my covenant

with God and to beg the prayers of this people that God will not leave me to myself, but help me (by the sufficient grace of Christ) to keep the covenant which I have made. And I intend to keep this paper by me, to help to remind me, to quicken me to duty and hinder me from sin, and to encourage me to go on cheerfully against temptations, looking still to Christ, who forsaketh not those that by faith and repentance come to him.

To all this let me add these considerations of the vanity of the creature and of all false hopes.

It is contrary to the nature of the creature [i.e., of created things] to be our peace; they are our discomforts and troubles, further than they help to lead us to the Creator. Let me not forget the time when I seemed near death. What comfort had I then in creatures? What ease from them? Was not all my hope in God? All creatures showed me that side of themselves on which vanity was written, and they had nothing that could satisfy my soul. Though I had as much mercy in means and friends as I could possibly desire, yet all this was nothing to me. The trouble of parting with them was much more than the comfort of enjoying them; and so it will be with me still, which should teach me to keep my heart loose from the creature and not over-love anything on this side heaven. Why should my heart be fixed where my home is not? Heaven is my home, God in Christ is all my happiness, and where my treasure is, there my heart should be. Come away, O my heart, from vanity; mount heavenward, and be not dead or dull if thou wouldst be free from trouble, and taste of real joy and pleasure. Hath not experience yet taught thee, that creature comforts, though they may be roses, have their pricks? Canst not thou be content to look on them and smell them at a distance, and covet no other use of them while thou art in the garden where they grow, and be content to leave them behind thee? If thou must needs have them in thy bosom, thou must scratch thy fingers to get them; and when thou hast them, though the smell awhile delight thee, they will quickly wither and are gone. Away then, O my carnal heart! retire to God, the only satisfying object. There mayest thou love without all danger of excess! Let thy love to God be fixed and transcendent. Amen.

Though these were the strivings of her heart towards God, her fears and troubles did not so pass away; settled peace of soul doth seldom come quickly to young converts, though their sincere resolutions may be settled. I find among her papers yet more of that day's work, following upon her subsequent examination and review. Bear with the length, if I transcribe it as I find it under her hand.

Christ saith: *In the world ye shall have trouble, in me ye shall have peace.* Something of both now I find at this time. This night, after returning thanks to God for my recovery, I find my heart sad, and trouble upon my spirit; and well it may be so, for the sins of this day have been very great. My heart hath not answered the expressions of thanks which have been uttered by the mouths of those that spake them to God. No! No, my heart hath not stirred and been drawn out towards my God! The thought of his love hath not ravished my soul. Alas! I scarce felt any holy spark to warm my soul this day. This day, which was a day of the greatest mercy of any in all my life, the day in which I have had an opportunity to give thanks for all the mercies of my life, and thanks itself is a greater mercy than the rest—all other mercies are to prepare for this. This is the work of a glorified saint, even a saint in heaven before the blessed face of God. It is his everlasting business to sing the songs of thanksgiving and praise to the Most High. But my thoughts have not been filled with the sweet foretastes of this blessed work which I might have had this day! O God! I beseech thee to forgive my sin and lay not my deadness to my charge, but overlook all my transgressions and look on me in Jesus Christ, my Savior. I am thine, Lord, and not mine own. This day I have under my hand and seal in the presence of witnesses, nay, in thine own presence (who art Witness sufficient, were there no eye to see me or ear to hear me), thou Lord that knowest all things, knowest that I have devoted my all to thee. Take it and accept my sacrifice. Help me to pay my vows! Wilt thou not accept me because I do it not more sincerely and believingly? O wilt thou strengthen my weak desires! I believe, Lord, help my unbelief. Thou that canst make me what I am not, O make me what thou wouldst have me be! In thee there is all fulness, and to thee I desire to come by Christ. Wilt thou now cast me off, because I do it not *unreservedly?* Lord, I confess the devil tempteth, and the flesh saith, *Spare something: What! let all go?* And I find in me a carnal selfish principle, ready to close with [i.e., give in to] the temptation. But thou canst prevent and conquer all, and speak death to these corruptions, and bid the tempter be gone. It is thy pleasure here to suffer thy dear children to be tempted; but suffer not temptations to prevail against thy Spirit and grace. If temptation be like a torrent of water to smother, quench, or hide the flame, yet wilt thou never let all the sparks of thy grace be put out in the soul where once thou hast truly kindled it. But Lord! suffer not such floods to fall in my soul, where the spark is so small already that it is even scarce discernible. O quicken it, and blow it up to a holy flame. Most gracious God! O do it here who hast done it for many a soul! O what have I said! that I have a spark of grace! why the least spark is worth ten thousand times more thanks than I can ever express! And I have been dead and unthankful, as is before confessed. And is that a sign of grace? Unthankful, dead, and dull have I been, and still am; but yet it must needs be from God's gift in me that I have any desires after him, and that this day I have desired to devote myself to him, and that I can say I would be more holy and more heavenly even as the Lord would have me be. Nay, I do not know the time when I had none of these desires and had no mind to God and the ways of godliness; and do I not know that there be many in this condition who have no desires after Christ and holiness? Here then is a matter of comfort given me from him that doth accept the desires of his poor creatures, even the Lord Christ, who will not quench the smoking flax nor break the bruised reed. I see then that I have yet matter of rejoicing, and must labor to be so humbled for my remaining sins, as may tend to my future joy in believing; but not so as to be discouraged and frightened from God, who is longsuffering and abundant in mercy. Rouse up thyself then to God, my soul. Humbly but believingly repent that thou hast been so unthankful and insensible of the benefits this day received. Up, up and lie not down so heavily; God hath heard prayers for thee and given thee life and opportunity to serve him. He hath given thee all the outward mercies thy heart can desire. He hath given thee dear, godly, able friends, such as can help thee in the way to heaven; yea, he hath set them to beg spiritual mercies for thee, who prevailed for temporal mercies for thee, and oft for many others; why then shouldst thou not watch and pray and wait in hope that he hath heard their prayers this day for thy soul, as formerly for thy body? They are things commanded of God to be asked, and we have his promise that seeking we shall find. It may be this night that many of God's dear children will yet pray for my soul. I doubt not some will, and shall I not be glad of such advantage? I heard this day that I must not forbear thanks, because the mercies are yet imperfect (else we should never give thanks on earth). Though therefore my grace be yet but a spark, and weak, my body weak, my heart sad, all these administer matter of thanks and praise as well as of supplication. Let me therefore keep close to both, they being the life of my life while I live here; and having daily need of supply from God, let me be daily with him and live as in his presence. Let him be the chief in all my thoughts, my heart and life. And let me remember to be earnest for my poor relations and dear friends, and the church and the people of God in general. And let me strive to keep such a moderate sense of sorrow in my soul, as occasion requireth. I have now cause of sorrow for parting with my dear friend, my father, my pastor.[13] He is by Providence called away, and going a long journey: What the Lord will do with him I cannot foresee. It may be he is preparing some great mercy for us and for his praise. I know not but such a day as this may be kept here on his account. The will of the Lord be done, for he is wise and good: We are his own, let him do with us what he pleaseth. All shall be for good to them that love God. I have cause to be humbled that I have been so unprofitable under mercies and means of grace; it may grieve me, now he is gone, that there is so little that came from him left upon my soul. O let this quicken and stir me up to be more diligent in the use of all the remaining helps and means. And if ever I should enjoy this mercy again, O let me make it appear that this night I was sensible of my neglect of it.

And now here is comfort, that I have to deal with a God of mercy that will hear a poor repenting sinner; a God that will in no wise cast out those that come to him, but loveth whom he loveth to the end. This is the God whom I have chosen and taken as my portion; the same God is his [i.e., Baxter's] God, his Guide and Comforter. The whole world is but a little house where God's children dwell a little while till he hath fitted them for the heavenly mansions. And if he send them out of one room into another to do his work and try their obedience, and if he put some in the darkest corners of his house to keep them humble, though he separate those that are most beloved of each other, it is only so that they may not love so much as to be loath to part and come to him who should have all their love. However it fareth with his children in this house (or howling wilderness), the time will come, and is at hand, when all the children shall be separate from the rebels, and be called home to dwell with their Father, their Head and Husband; and the elect shall be gathered into one. Then farewell sorrow, farewell hard heart! farewell tears and sad repentance! And then blessed saints that have believed and obeyed! Never so unworthy, crowned thou must be! This was the project of redeeming love! When the Lord shall take our carcases from the grave, and make us shine as the sun in glory; then, then shall friends meet and never part, and remember their sad and weary nights and days no more! Then may we love freely! What now is wanting to dispel all sorrow from my heart? Nothing but the greater hopes that I shall be one of this number. This, this can do it. No matter if I had no friend near me, and none on earth; if God be not far from me, it's well enough; and whatever here befalls the church and people of God, it's but as for one day, and presently the storm will be all over. Let me therefore cast all my care on God. Let me wait on him in the way of duty, and trust him; let me run with patience the race that is set before me, looking to Jesus, the Author and Finisher of my faith, and believingly go to him in all my troubles; and let me so labor here, that I may find rest to my soul in the rest that remaineth for the people of God.[14]

Rest! O sweet word! The weary shall have rest, they shall rest in the Lord.

April 10[15] on Thursday night at twelve of the clock; a day and night never to be forgotten by the least of all God's mercies, yea, less than the least, thy unworthy, unthankful, hardhearted creature.

M. Charlton

Is not here in all these papers (which I saw not till she was dead) a great deal of work for one day, besides all the public work of a thanksgiving day? If I should give you an account of all her following twenty-one years, what a volume would it amount to! If you ask why I recite all this, which is but matter well known to ordinary Christians, I answer: It is not a matter of knowledge, but of soul workings toward God. Is not this extraordinary in a convert of a year or few months standing? The love of God, and her, makes me think it worth the publishing. They that think otherwise may pass it by, but there are souls to whom it will be savory and profitable.

Yet she continued under great fears that she had not saving grace because she had not that degree of holy affection which she desired; and before in her sickness, her fears increased her disease and danger. I will here, for the use of others in the like case, recite some scraps of a letter of counsel as I find them transcribed by herself.

I advise you to set more effectually to the means of your necessary consolation; your strange silent keeping your case to yourself (from your mother, and all your friends) is an exceeding injury to your peace. Is it God, or Satan, that hindereth you from opening [i.e., disclosing] your sore ... and make you think that concealment is your wisdom? If it be pride that forbids it, how dare you obey such a commander? Many of our sores are half healed when well opened. If prudence foresees some forbidding inconvenience, you have prudent friends, and two prudent persons may see more than one. But because you will not tell us, I will disjunctively [i.e., in either-or terms] tell it you.

Your trouble of soul is either some affliction, or some sin, or the doubt of your sincerity and true grace.

If it be affliction, dare you so indulge impatience as to give up your hope of future comforts, while you have God's love and title to salvation? Dare you say that these are of so small weight that a cross like yours will weigh them down? and that you will not rejoice in all the promises of life eternal, till your cross be removed?

If it be sin, it is either past or present; if past, why do you not repent and thankfully accept your pardon? If present, it is inward corruption or outward transgression. Whichever it be, if you love it, why do you grieve for it and groan under it? If you grieve for it, why are you not willing to leave it and be holy? If you are willing to leave it, and would fain have God's grace in the use of his means to make you holy, this is the true nature of repentance. And why then are you not thankful for grace received, for pardon, adoption, and your part in Christ, more than you are troubled for remaining in sin? Should none rejoice that have sin to trouble them and keep them in a daily watch and war? Read Romans 7 and 8, if you will see the contrary: *If any man sin, we have an Advocate with the Father, Jesus Christ the righteous, and he is the propitiation for our sins.* Dare you refuse your comforts on such reasons as would deny comfort to all the world? He that saith he hath no sin is a liar; and will you for this deny the known duty of thanks and praise for all that you have received? You have been taught to differentiate between cause of doubting and cause of filial humiliation. And if it were any particular sin that needs particular help and counsel, why do you not open it for help (which probably would do more against it, than many years' secret trouble and dejection alone will do)?

If it be doubts of your sincerity and grace, why do you refuse to reason the case and say what it is that persuadeth you that you are graceless, that we may try it by the Word of God?

What evidence is it that you want? You have confessed that sometimes you are convinced of your sincerity; and can you so easily deny what you have found as to conclude yourself so miserable as you do? Should all do thus that have not constant apprehensions of their evidence, and whose assurance is hindered by imperfections? You have heard the contrary.

But suppose that you have yet no saving grace or part in Christ, why stand you complaining while Christ stands intreating you to accept his mercy? Is he not in good earnest? The offer is free; it is not your purchase and merit, but consent that will prove your title. Why do you complain and not consent even to the baptismal covenant? Or if you consent, why do you complain as if Christ's promise were not true, or as if consent were not a proof of saving faith? If you confess that you should not doubt and be dejected on such terms, methinks the cure should be half wrought. Dare you indulge it while you know it to be your sin? Have you not sin enough already? And is it not unkindness to deny so great a mercy as the converting grace which you so lately felt, and to suspect his love who is love itself and hath so largely expressed his love to you? Would you easily believe that your mother would kill you for such defects as you fear that God will damn you for? Yea, though she were perfectly just and holy? Is it consistent to hear ministers tell men that Christ beseecheth them to be reconciled to God and will refuse none that are willing of his grace and cure, and at the same time to hear such as you almost willing to despair, as if God would not be reconciled, nor give grace to them that fain would have it, but will be inclined to reject humbled souls?

Reason not for your distrustful fears and sorrows, but

constantly disown them and accuse them, and then they will vanish by degrees and die: Yea, then you will sure oppose them yourself and God will help you. Can you look that God should help you against the sin which you plead for and defend? If faith and love be the vital graces, distrust of God and denying of his love must not be defended as no sin. As the ungodly cannot expect the grace which they refuse, so how can you expect the peace which you oppose, and say as Psalm 77: *My soul refuseth to be comforted,* and say of your passionate fear and grief, as Jonah of his anger: *I do well to be angry, even unto death?* Be convinced that Christ is yours, if you accept him and consent, and then that comfort is your interest, right, and duty; and then you will do more to comfort yourself than I am endeavoring when I chide you for your fears. Sure sinful sorrow is no desirable thing, nor to be pleaded for. You durst do nothing to the murder of a friend, no, nor to his grief; and you are bid to love your neighbor as yourself; away then with your weakening griefs and troubles, lest they prove a degree of self-murder. If you care for yourself, the comfort of your mother and friends, and the honor of the unspeakable riches of God's grace, at least own it to be your duty to oppose sinful fear, to rejoice in God and serve him with delight and cheerful praises, and to do your best against all that is against this duty. And suffer not your sore to fester by your silence, but open your case to someone who is able to help you impartially to try it by the Word of God and to pray with you that God will mercifully show you your infirmities and the remedy. It would be wisdom to conceal your case from others only if you could well be cured without their help.

Some strivings against her fears and sorrows I find next in this paper following, dated by her April third.[16]

The sadder my present condition is, the greater is the mercy that I am yet alive: Why then should I not give God thanks for that, and beg the rest which yet I want? And though my life seem but a burden to me sometimes, it is my great mistake; for the greatest afflictions are nothing to hell-torments. Were they as great as ever any had, while I am alive on this side eternity, there is hope. The time of grace is yet continued; if I be found in mercy's way, I know not but God may yet be gracious, and give me my soul as he hath done my life at his people's prayers. For I cannot but look on my life as an answer of their prayers. And surely they desired my life only that I might live to God. I desired it myself on no other terms. It was my earnest request that I might not live, if not to him. Why then should I be persuaded by Satan to think that God will not give me grace as well as life? May I not rather be encouraged with patience to wait for further mercy? It is a mercy that I am in any measure more aware of my danger and have any desire to be holy. I will therefore stir up my soul to thankfulness and be humbled that I can be no more thankful. I will acknowledge the mercy I have received and the probability of future mercy, and this by God's assistance the devil shall not hinder me from doing.

I will add one of her papers containing her resolutions after her recovery in some few particulars.

December 30 was my worst day. I did not then think to be alive this day: I ought not to forget it. On Jan. 1, *New Year's Day*, I first bled at the nose largely and after mended. The fourth day was kept in humiliation for me. April 10 was set as a day of thanksgiving.

When I thought I should die, I was more than ordinarily aware of my unprofitable life, and had such convictions as usually people in my condition have; and I then made many resolutions as in such cases others do. I had remembered that I had heard much of the promises that many made in sickness, which they never performed; and I thought it was gross hypocrisy to speak now of that which I was past performing (as I thought), but that I had better write down my purposes and announce them if God recovered me, that they might be as strong an engagement on me as if I had spoken them to men.

I. I resolved that I would endeavor to get and keep a sense of that great mercy of God's restoring me from the peril of threatened death in answer of prayers, which was the greater in that God threatened to take me hence when I was but in the birth and had scarce well begun to live. This mercy I promised to be thankful for, and to acknowledge other mercies as God should make me able.

II. I resolved that I would endeavor to be in a fixed state and way of duty; and in order to this, I would take advice of one who is (I conceive) most fit to advise me.[17] And I resolved by God's assistance, that I will not consult with flesh and blood nor study my carnal interest, but resolvedly set on the way of duty and freely discourse my thoughts, so far as is requisite to my just advice. And that I will speak my reasons and heart-risings against any thing that is propounded to me which I judge unmeet. And I resolved when I saw my duty, cheerfully to do it, and keep a sense of the sweetness and obligations of God's love and mercy.

III. I resolved to pray and labor for a true sense of the sins of this nation in general, and in particular of the sins of my relations and of my own. And that till it please God to give me cause of rejoicing on the behalf of my relations and of my own soul's recovery and spiritual welfare, I will continue with humiliation to supplicate the Lord. And though I would not shut out a greater duty by a lesser, yet I will avoid all manner of feastings as much as I well can, and all noxious, sensual delights; and when I must be present, I will use some mortifying restraint. And this I would do in my habit, and all other things, but that I would lay no snare on myself by renouncing what occasions may oblige me to, but by all means I would strive to keep upon my heart a sense of my friends' danger and my own.

IV. I resolve, if Providence concur, to go to London as soon as I can after the day of thanksgiving, for the reasons mentioned in another place.

What these reasons were I find not. This following fragment of hers hints something of it:

I begin already to be aware of my misusing the helps which God had given me. I know now how I should love ordinances and means of grace, and to what end: not to break my heart when Providence removeth them from me or me from them, but I should love them for God and use them for him, and expect my greatest comfort from him and not from men and means themselves. This is no more than what I thought I had known long ago, but I never knew it indeed till now. And now I do but begin to know it. When I felt my heart ready to sink under a burden of sorrow, God was pleased to ask me what I ailed? Was my condition worse than ever? Had I less hopes of his love than heretofore? If not, why do I mourn more than when I lay under that curse? What is it that I have chosen for my hope and happiness? Is that lost and gone? Am I left in such a place and case as God cannot be found in if I truly seek him? or that God cannot sweeten with his presence? If not, why do I not contentedly thank God for what I have already had? I cannot say it's better that I had never had it than now to leave it. No, I must be willing to submit to God and be humbled in the sense of my abuse of mercy, so far as it may quicken me to diligence for the time to come. And if ever God more trust me with such treasure as once I had, I will strive to show that I better know the worth of it than I did before. My thoughts often tell me that if I were but in a condition in which I had opportunity to serve God with more cost to the flesh than here I do, it would either show my hypocrisy or give me more assuring evidence that I am indeed sincere.

And it is a useful note that I find added to this by her:

If my trouble be for my sin, my care will be more for the removing of my sin than of the affliction.

And if God should take away the affliction it would not content me, unless sin be taken away and my heart amended.

If it be sin that I am troubled for, it will be my great care not to sin in my trouble.

And if it be my sin that troubleth me, I have the more cause to submit to God's hand and silently bear the punishment of my iniquity. It shameth murmuring when we truly look on sin the cause, though it bring the wholesome sorrow of repentance.

And if I mourn for fear lest God be departing, I should seek him and cleave the closer to him and not depart from God, and then he will not depart from me.

Four

Some Parcels of Counsel for Her Deliverance from This Distressed Case, Which I Find Reserved by Her for Her Use

[THE DOCUMENTS MAKING UP THIS CHAPTER ARE MOSTLY
EXTRACTS FROM RICHARD'S PASTORAL LETTERS TO
MARGARET, COPIED OUT BY HER FOR HER OWN LONG-TERM
REFLECTION. GOD-CENTEREDNESS, AND REALIZATION OF THE
LOVE AND FAITHFULNESS OF THE LORD JESUS CHRIST, AND
LESS SELF-ABSORPTION, AND MORE ACCEPTANCE OF PRESENT
CIRCUMSTANCES ARE THE MAIN EMPHASES OF RICHARD'S
EXHORTATIONS.]

WHILE IN HER LANGUISHING, AND AFTER IT, she was still cast down, condemning herself as a graceless wretch; and her good mother and friends were afraid that her grief would increase her sickness as it did their sadness. And yet she obstinately concealed it from all, save a few sad complaints to one person[18] who wrote thereof some fragments which she extracted for her use. I shall here recite them for others that have the same fears.

The miscarriage of a relation troubling her, this was set down:

When God hath done so much for you, will you leave it in the power of an unconstant creature to trouble you and rob you of your peace? Is the joy of the Holy Ghost so subject to the malice of your enemies or the weakness of your friends? Delight yourself in an all-sufficient constant God, and he will be to you a sufficient constant delight, and will give you the desires of your heart. I see you are yet imperfect in self-denial, while you are too aware of unkindnesses and crosses from your friends and bear them with too much passion and weakness. Know you not yet what the creature is, and how little is to be expected from it? Do you not still reckon to meet with such infirmities in the best, as will be injurious to others as they are troublesome to themselves? It's God that we most wrong, and yet he beareth with us; and so must we with one another. Had you expected that creatures should deal as creatures, and sinners as sinners, how little of this kind of trouble had you felt? Especially take heed of too much regard to matters of reputation and the thoughts of men; else you are like a leaf in the wind that will have no rest. Look on man as nothing, and be content to approve yourself to God; and then so much honor as is good for you will follow as the shadow. If every frailty and unkindness of the best friends must be your trouble, it is to be impatient with the unavoidable depravity of mankind; and you may as well grieve that they were born in sin, and make your acquaintance. And it [i.e., each such experience] should be used as a mercy to keep you from inordinate affections to friends. It's a mercy to be driven from relying on created things for contentment though it be by enemies. Keep a fixed apprehension of the inconsiderableness of all these things that cross you, and turn your eye to God, to Christ, to heaven, the things of unspeakable weight, and you will have no room for these childish troubles.

Yet turn not the discovery of this your weakness into dejection, but amendment. I perceive you are apter to hold to the sense of your own distempers than to think what counsel is given you against them.

On another occasion she recorded these words:

How hard it is to keep our hearts from going too far even in honest affections toward the creature, while we are so backward to love God, who should have all the heart and soul and might. Too strong love to any, though it be good in the kind, may be sinful and hurtful in the degree. It will turn too many of your thoughts from God, and they will be too often running after the beloved creature. And by this exercise of thoughts and affections on the creature, it may divert and cool your love to God which will not be kept up, unless your thoughts be more to him, yea though it be for his sake that you love them. It will increase your sufferings by involving you in all the dangers and troubles of those whom you over-love.

When she seemed to herself near death:

You now see what the world and all its pleasures are, and how it would have used you, if you had had no better a portion and God had not taught you a happier choice. Providence now tells you that they are vanity, and if over-valued, worse; but if you learn to see their nothingness, you will be above the trouble of losing them, as well as the snares of too delightful enjoying them. Pardon all injuries to men and turn your thoughts from them; and keep your heart as near as possible to the heart of Christ, and live as in his arms, who is usually sweetest when the creature most faileth us, if we do but turn our hearts from it to him.

Another time:

Can you find that you are resolvedly devoted to Christ, and yet doubt whether Christ be resolvedly and surely yours? Are you willinger or faithfuller than he?

Hence she gathered herself as followeth:

When I read the evidence of my self-resignation to Christ, I should as it were see Christ standing over me with the tenderest care, and hear him say, *I accept thee as my own.* For I must believe his acceptance as I perform my resignation. O what is he providing for me? What entertainment with him shall I shortly find? Not such as he found with man, when he came to seek us. It is not a manger, a crown of thorns, a cross, that he is preparing for me: When I have had my part of these in following him, I shall have my place in the glorious Jerusalem.

This fragment she wrote next:

For the sake of your own soul and life and friends, and for the honor of that tender mercy and free grace which you are bound to magnify, let not Satan get advantage against your peace and thankfulness to God and the acknowledgment of his obliging love. Let him not on pretense of humiliation turn your eyes on a weak distempered heart, from the unspeakable mercy which should fill your heart with love and joy, notwithstanding all your lamented infirmities. You perceive not that it is Satan that would keep you still under mournful sadness, under the pretense of repentance and godly sorrow. You are not acquainted with his wiles. You have cause of sorrow, but much more of joy. And your rejoicing in God's love would please him better than all your sad complaints and troubles, though he despise not a contrite spirit. I charge it on your conscience [i.e., command you], that when you are in prayer you confess and lament your distrustful, suspicious, unthankful, uncomfortable thoughts of God and Jesus Christ, more than all your want of sorrow for him. And you trouble yourself for such kind of sins, the honesty of whose occasion may give you more comfort than the fault doth sorrow. I know we have not our comfort at command. But see that your endeavor and striving be more for a comfortable than for a sorrowful frame of spirit.

Two things I must blame you for. 1. That you take the imperfections of your duties and obedience to be greater reasons for discomfort than the performance and sincerity are reasons for comfort, as if you thought anything were perfect here or that it were better to do nothing than do it imperfectly, or as if you would have no comfort till you can perform such duty and obedience as hath no need of pardon and a Savior; and so no man living might have any comfort in anything that he doth.

2. That when unreasonable fears and troubles are upon you, and troubling thoughts are still upon your mind, you say that you cannot help it nor turn your thoughts away to anything else. I know you have not an absolute power over your thoughts, but some you have. Why else hath God made a law for our thoughts and laid so much duty on them and forbidden their sin so much? Much may be done, if you will be resolute.

Think whether Christ came from the Father to bring tidings of sadness and despair, or of great joy; and whether angels preached not Glory to God in the highest, on earth peace and to men good will? And whether faith, hope, and love, which are the things which Christ will work on souls, be not more powerful to destroy your sins than despair or discouragement of mind?

And because you complain so much of sin, I ask you why doth not your conscience more accuse you of the sin of unthankful denying or extenuating the mercies of God, and no more magnifying them? And for overlooking so much the meritorious righteousness of Christ, while you complain for want of more of your own? I would not deceive you by telling you that you need none in yourself and that all your righteousness is out of you in Christ: I know that your righteousness must exceed that of the Pharisees, and the unrighteous shall not inherit the Kingdom of God, and he that doth righteousness is righteous. But at what bar or tribunal? Only at that of grace, which supposeth the reconciling, pardoning righteousness of Christ. It is not at the bar of rigorous justice according to the law, which requireth innocence to justification; there Christ only is your righteousness, and you have none and must dream of none but that which floweth from his and stands in subordination to it and is your title to it and improvement of it, even your thankful accepting a free-given Savior, Head and Lord, and pardon and the Spirit to sanctify you more and fit you for communion with God and for glory. Esteem most, choose first, and seek most the love of God the Father, the grace of Christ, and the communion of the Holy Ghost, and this subordinate righteousness will certainly prove the meritorious perfect righteousness of Christ to be for you, instead of a perfect righteousness of your own. There is no defect in his sacrifice or merits. If you lacked a title to Christ you were unjustified; but none wants that who consenteth to his covenant, as before; and that consent you cannot deny. Will you live like a forsaken orphan exposed in a wilderness, while God's tender love is saving you, and Christ is glorying in you as the fruit of his blood, and the angels of God are serving you and rejoicing at your conversion? I entreat you think whether it be not the great work that God hath called you to do, to honor his grace and propagate to all about you, as you are able, a joyful, thankful, hoping, and praising frame of soul, and to stir up all the delightful praise of God? As ministers must do it by preaching, all must do it by conference and example. And is your dejected sadness the performance of this?

When she desired to be prayed for, she wrote down this answer which I find now in her papers:

It is well if you know what prayer to put up, or what to desire. I'll pray for you according to the best of my judgments; and I'll tell you for what, that you may know what to pray for for yourself. First, I'll pray that your thoughts may be turned to the magnifying of God's love, that you may remember that he is as good as he is great, and that you may be more conscious of his mercy than of your own unworthiness. I'll pray that you may have so lively an apprehension of your everlasting felicity, as may make you long to be with Christ; and that you may have more self-denial and that humility which makes you little in your own eyes. That you may be much less tender and liable to commotion and disquiet of mind, and less conscious of unkindnesses and of bodily dangers and of sin itself, while the sense of it hinders the sense of mercy. A meek and a quiet and patient spirit is of great price in the sight of God. I will pray that you may be delivered from too much inward passion, of fear, grief, or discontent. I will pray that no creature may seem greater, better, or more regardable or necessary to you than it is; and that you would look on all as walking shadows, vanity, and liars (that is, untrusty) further than you can see God in them, or they lead you up to him; that they never be over-loved, over-feared, over-trusted, or their thoughts too much regarded. Above all, I'll pray that you may be less self-willed, and not be too passionately or unmovably set upon the fulfilling of all your will; but may have a will that is compliant with the will of God and can change as he would have it, and will follow him and not run before him; and can endure to be crossed and denied by God and man without discomposedness and impatient trouble of mind. I shall pray that seeming wisdom may not entangle you, either in the concealment of anything which greatly needeth your friends' advice, or in the hiding of your talents by unprofitable silence as to all good conversation, because of the enmity which you have to hypocrisy; and that you will not live in sins of omission for fear of seeming better than you are. By this you may know wherein I think you faulty.

The next I find is this advice against her resolution to go to London.

It is not lawful to speak an idle word, and especially deliber-
ately; much less to go an idle journey. What if you fall sick by
the way, or some weakness take you there, will not conscience ask you who called you hither? Your weakness of
spirit, that cannot endure this or that at home with your
dearest friends, is so far below the quiet composed fortitude
which you should have, that you ought not to give way to it.
If you are really at the command of your impatience, how are
you obedient to the command of God? It is a greater work
to bring your mind and will to the will of God than to
change place or apparel or run away as Jonah in discontent.
O for a mind and will that need no more to quiet it than to
know what is the will of God and our duty, and in every
estate therewith to be content. When you know your duty,
do it resolutely and cheerfully, and scorn to run away and
turn your back, that you may do it without censure where
you are unknown. Use well the means God here vouchsafes
you, and do your duty with a quiet mind, and *follow God* in
your removes.

Much more of such counsels she transcribed, but I forbear
reciting more. She ends those papers with these words:

The best creature-affections have a mixture of some creature-
imperfections, and therefore need some gall to wean us from
the faulty part. God must be known to be God, our rest, and
therefore the best creature to be but a creature! O miserable
world (how long must I continue in it? And why is this
wretched heart so loath to leave it) where we can have no fire
without smoke, and our dearest friends must be our greatest

grief; and when we begin in hope and love and joy, before we are aware, we fall into an answerable measure of distress. Learn by experience, when any condition is inordinately or excessively sweet to thee, to say, *From hence must be my sorrow.* (O how true!)

Five

Her Temper, Occasioning These Troubles of Mind

[RICHARD, AS PASTOR-WIDOWER, DESCRIBES MARGARET'S TEMPERAMENT AS A YOUNG CHRISTIAN AND THEREAFTER. SHE WAS RESERVED, INTENSE, HIGHLY STRUNG, RESTLESS, ARDENT, FEARFUL, PASSIONATE AND PERFECTIONIST, SAD AND SELF-CONDEMNING. SHE EXPERIENCED RECURRING HEADACHES (MIGRAINES?), BUT NOT THE KIND OF DEPRESSION ("MELAN-CHOLY") THAT IMPEDES RATIONAL THOUGHT.]

THE SOUL WHILE IN THE BODY works much according to the body's disposition. She was of an extraordinary sharp and piercing wit. She had a natural reservedness and secrecy, increased by thinking it necessary prudence not to be open; by which means she was oft misunderstood by her nearest friends, and consequently often crossed and disappointed by those that would have pleased her. And as she could understand people much by their looks and hints, so she expected all should know her mind without expressing it, which bred her frustrations and discontents. And she had a natural tenderness and troubledness of mind upon the crossing of her just desires: too quick and ungovernable a sense of displeasing words or deeds. She had a diseased, unresistable fearfulness; her quick and too sensitive nature was over-timorous. And to increase it, she said she was four times, before I knew her, in danger of death, of which one was by the smallpox. And more to increase it, her mother's house,[19] being a garrison, it was stormed whilst she was in it, and part of the housing about it burnt, and men lay killed before her face. And all of them were threatened and stripped of their clothing so that they were obliged to borrow clothes. And the great work upon her soul, in her conversion, moved all her passions. And then her dangerous sickness, and the sentence of death to so young a convert, must needs be a very awaking thing; and coming on her before she had any assurance of her justification, it did increase her fear. And in this state of mind she lived in the churchyard side, where she saw all the burials of the dead, and kept a death's head [i.e., skull] in her closet always before her. And other such mortifying spectacles increased her sad disposition.

And the excessive love which she had to her mother did much increase her grief when she expected death.

Though she called it melancholy that by all this she was cast into, yet it rather seemed a partly natural and a partly adventitious diseased fearfulness in a tender over-passionate nature, that had no power to quiet her own fears, without any other cloud on her understanding.

And all was much increased by her wisdom so stifling all the appearance of it, that it all inwardly wrought and had no ease by vent.

And having keen spirits and thin sharp blood, she had a strong hemicrania or headache once a month and oft once a fortnight, or more, from the age of fifteen or sixteen years. All these together much tended to hinder her from a quiet and comfortable temper.

And in a word, all the operations of her soul were very intense and strong; strong wit, and strong love, and strong displeasure. And when God showed her what holiness was, she thought she must presently have it in so great a degree as the ripest saints do here attain; and that because she had not as much heavenly life and sense and delight in God as she knew she should have and desired, she concluded of it that she had none that was sincere.

One of the first things by which her change was discovered to her mother and her friends was her fervent, secret prayers; for, living in a great house of which the middle part was ruined by the [Civil] wars, she chose a closet in the further end, where she thought none heard her. But some that overheard her said they never heard so fervent prayers from any person.

Yet she desired me to draw up a form suited to her own condition, which I did, and find it now reserved among her papers; but I cannot tell whether she ever used it, having affections and freedom of expression without it. I had thought to have annexed it for the use of afflicted penitents, but it will be but a digression in this narrative.

Six

Of Our Marriage and Our Habitations

[MARRIAGE TO RICHARD MEANT A SOCIAL AND FINANCIAL COMEDOWN FOR MARGARET, BUT SHE TOOK THIS IN STRIDE, FINDING GREAT FULFILLMENT IN MARRIED LIFE AS SHE LAID HERSELF OUT TO SUPPORT RICHARD AND HELP OTHERS BOTH MATERIALLY AND SPIRITUALLY. SHE ACCEPTED CONSTANT CHANGES OF RESIDENCE WITHOUT COMPLAINT, HANDLING EACH NEW DOMESTIC SITUATION BEAUTIFULLY, EVEN WHEN IT MEANT JOINING HER HUSBAND IN PRISON.]

THE UNSUITABLENESS OF OUR AGE, and my former known purposes against marriage, and against the conveniency of ministers' marriage, who have no sort of necessity, made our marriage the matter of much public talk and wonder. And the true opening of her case and mine, and the many strange occurrences which brought it to pass, would take away the wonder of her friends and mine that knew us; and the notice would much conduce to the understanding of some other passages of our lives. Yet wise friends, by whom I am advised, think it better to omit such personal particularities at least at this time. Both in her case and mine, there was much extraordinary, which it doth not much concern the world to be acquainted with. From the first thoughts of it, many changes and stoppages intervened, and long delays, till I was silenced and ejected with many hundreds more, and so being separated from my old pastoral charge, which was enough to take up all my time and labor, some of my dissuading reasons were then over. And at last on September 10, 1662, we were married in St. Benet-Fink

Church, by Mr. Samuel Clark (yet living), having been before contracted by Mr. Simeon Ash, both in the presence of Mr. Henry Ashurst and Mrs. Ash.[20]

She consented to these conditions of our marriage. That I would have nothing that before our marriage was hers, that I (who wanted no outward supplies) might not seem to marry her for covetousness. That she would so alter her affairs, that I might be entangled in no lawsuits. That she would expect none of my time which my ministerial work should require.

When we were married, her sadness and melancholy vanished: Counsel did something to it, and contentment something; and being taken up with our household affairs did somewhat. And we lived in inviolated love and mutual complacency conscious of the benefit of mutual help. These near nineteen years I know not that we ever had any breach in the point of love or point of interest, save only that she somewhat grudged that I had persuaded her for my quietness to surrender so much of her estate, as disabled her from helping others so much as she earnestly desired. But that even this was not from a covetous mind is evident by these instances. Though her portion (which was £2,000 besides that given up aforesaid) was (by ill-debtors) £200 lost in her mother's time and £200 after, before her marriage, and all she had reduced to almost £1,650, yet she never grudged at anything that the poverty of debtors deprived her of.

She had before been acquainted with the Lord Chancellor's offering me a bishopric; and though it might have taken off the censure of those relations that thought that she debased herself in marrying me, and also might have seemed good to her for the wealth as well as the honors, she was so far from desiring my accepting it, that I am persuaded had I done it, it would have alienated her much from me in point of esteem and love. Not that she had any opinion against the episcopacy then (that ever I could perceive), but that she abhorred a worldly, mercenary mind in a minister of Christ and was a sharp censurer of all that for gain or honor or worldly ends should stretch their consciences to anything that they thought God forbade. I am assured (though toward her end she wished she had been abler to relieve the needy and do more good), that she lived a far more contented life in our mean condition, even when she stooped to receive from others that had been strangers to her, than she would have done had I been a bishop and she had had many thousands pounds more at her disposal; yea, I am persuaded she would not have easily endured it.

Another trial of her wealth and honor was when I and all such others were cast out of all possession and hope of all ecclesiastical maintenance; she was not ignorant of the scorn and the jealousies and wrath and persecutions that I was likely to be exposed to; yea, she had heard and seen it already begun by Bishop Morley[21] forbidding me to preach before, and preaching himself, and his dean [i.e., the clergyman in charge of Worcester cathedral] and many others fiercely against me in Kidderminster pulpit; she had quickly heard them that were cast out and silenced, deeply accused as if they had deserved it. To choose a participation of such a life that had no encouragement from any worldly wealth or honor, yea, that was exposed to such certain suffering which had no end in prospect on this side death, did show that she was far from covetousness. Much more evidence of this I shall show you as it falls in its place.

Among other troubles that her marriage exposed her to, one was our oft necessitated removals [i.e., moves to different houses or towns], which to those that must take houses and bind themselves to landlords and fit and furnish them is more than for single persons that have no such clogs or cares. First we took a house in Moorfields, after at Acton; next that, another at Acton, and after that another there; and after that we were put to one of the former again; and after that to diverse others in another place and county, as followeth. And the women have most of that sort of trouble, but she easily bare it all.

And I know not that ever she came to any place where she did not extraordinarily win the love of the inhabitants (unless in any street where she stayed so short a time as not to be known to them). Had she had but the riches of the world to have done the good that she had a heart to do, how much would she have been loved, who in her mean and low condition won so much?

And her behavior in public won more love than her liberality; she could not endure to hear one give another any sour, rough, or hasty word. Her speech and countenance was always kind and civil, whether she had anything to give or not.

And all her kindness tended to some better end than barely to relieve people's bodily wants, even to oblige or to deliver them from some straits which filled them with hurtful care and became a matter of great temptation to them. If she could hire the poor to hear God's Word from Conformist or Nonconformist, or to read good serious practical books, whether written by Conformists or Nonconformists, it answered her end and desire, and many an hundred books hath she given to those ends. But of these things more hereafter. This is here but to answer the foresaid objection, and to lead on to the following particular passages of her life.

While I was at Acton, her carriage and charity so won the people there, that all I ever heard of greatly esteemed and loved her. And she, being earnestly desirous of doing good, prepared her house for the reception of those that would come in to be instructed by me between the morning and evening public assemblies, and after. And the people that had never been used to such things, accounted worldly ignorant persons, gave us great hopes of their edifications and reformation, and filled the room and went with me also into the church (which was at my door). And when I was afterward removed, the people hearing that I again wanted a house (being ten miles off), they unanimously subscribed a request to me to return to my old house with them and offered to pay my house rent, which I took kindly; and it was much her winning behavior which thus won their love.

When I was carried thence to the common jail for teaching them, as aforesaid, I never perceived her trouble at it. She cheerfully went with me into prison; she brought her best bed thither and did much to remove the removable inconveniences of the prison. I think she scarce ever had a pleasanter time in her life than while she was with me there. And whereas people upon such occasions were not unapt to be liberal, it was against her mind to receive more than necessity required. Only three persons gave me just as much as paid lawyers and prison charges, and when one offered me more, she would not receive it. But all was far short of the great charges of our removal to another habitation.

The Parliament making a new sharper law against us, I was forced to remove into another county.[22] Thither she went with me and removed her goods that were removable from Acton to Totteridge, being engaged for the rent of the house we left. At Totteridge, the first year, few poor people are put to the hardness that she was put to. We could have no house but part of a poor farmer's, where the chimneys so extremely smoked as greatly annoyed her health; for it was a very hard winter, and the coal smoke so filled the room that we were all day sat in that it was as a cloud, and we were even suffocated with the stink. And she had ever a great constriction of the lungs that could not bear smoke or closeness. This was the greatest bodily suffering that her outward condition put her to, which was increased by my continual pain there. But her charity to her poor landlady set her son apprentice, who now liveth well.

Thence we removed to a house, which we took to ourselves, which required so great alterations and amendment as took her up much time and labor; and to her great comfort she got Mr. Corbet and his wife to dwell with us. And in all these changes and troubles she lived in great peace.

When the King's Declarations and Licences gave Noncon-formists leave to build meeting-places and preach,[23] she was against my going to London till others were there settled, lest I should anticipate them and gather any auditors who would else go to others, especially their old ejected pastors, but when others were settled, she was earnest with me to go for the exercise of my ministry.

Upon our remove to London, out of tender regard to my health, which she thought the situation might contribute much unto,[24] she chose and took for us this most pleasant and convenient house in Southampton Square, where she died. These were our removes.

Seven

Of Her Exceeding Desires to Do Good

[MARGARET FACILITATED RICHARD'S MINISTRY AND FUR-
THERED THE GOSPEL EVERY WAY SHE COULD. SHE HIRED
ROOMS FOR PREACHING, BUILT A CHAPEL, STARTED A SCHOOL,
RECRUITED SUPPLY PREACHERS, RAISED AND DISBURSED LARGE
SUMS FOR CHARITY, AND MORE. HER INITIATIVE IN COMMAN-
DEERING A CARPENTER WHEN A BEAM CRACKED KEPT THE
FLOOR OF AN UPSTAIRS ROOM WHERE RICHARD WAS PREACH-
ING FROM A FATAL COLLAPSE. HER ZEAL SOMETIMES LED HER
INTO UNWISE DECISIONS AND STRAINED HER RESOURCES TO
THE UTMOST. WHILE KEEPING RICHARD ACTIVE IN THE PUL-
PIT WITHOUT SALARY, SHE CRITICIZED NONCONFORMING
CLERGY WHO FEARED ARREST AND COMPLAINED OF WANT,
AND SHE DISAGREED WITH RICHARD'S ATTEMPTS TO EASE
YOUNG MEN'S PASSAGE INTO ORDAINED MINISTRY, LEST THEY
PROVE HYPOCRITES, JUST AS SHE DISAGREED WITH HIS RELUC-
TANCE TO BORROW MONEY FOR CHARITABLE PURPOSES.]

AS AT HER CONVERSION AND IN HER SICKNESS she absolutely devoted herself and all that she had to God, so she earnestly set herself to perform it to the last. At first she gave but the tenth of her
incomes to the poor; but I quickly convinced her that God must
not be stinted, but as all was his, so all must be used for him by his
stewards, and of all we must give account. Only in his appointed
order we must use it, which is: 1. For our own natural necessities.
2. For public necessary good. 3. For the necessities of our children
and such relations as are part of our charge. 4. And then for the

godly poor. 5. And then for the common poor's necessities. 6. And lastly, for conveniences, but nothing for unuseful things.

To name the particular great instances of her private charity is neither suitable to my ends nor her desires. I will instance but some of her more public cares.

She was earnestly desirous of the winning of souls and of the utmost improvement of mine and other men's labors to that end. At Acton, I told you how she promoted it; and at Totteridge, out of church time, she gladly opened her doors to her neighbors that would come in for instruction.

At London, when she saw me too dull and backward to seek any employment till I was called, and that most places in the city had some supplies, she first fished out of me in what place I most desired more preaching. I told her in St. Martin's Parish,[25] where are said to be forty thousand more than can come into the church, especially among all the new buildings in St. James', where neighbors many live like Americans [i.e., native Americans of pagan faith] and have heard no sermon of many years.

When she had once heard this, without my knowledge she set one to seek after some capacious room there; and none was found, but diverse rooms over the market-house laid together. She got one to take them. And they two agreed to importune me to preach each morning, and in the afternoon to get by turns the ablest ministers they could procure in London. And to that end she got a minister an hundred miles off to come up and help me, promising him £40 a year to go from day to day to supply the places of such eminent ministers as should be got. All this charge, besides paying a clerk and a woman to look to the seats, rose high. Part of it the people paid, and the rest she paid herself.

Hence God was pleased to remove us, but by the interposition of a marvelous deliverance. The roof of that market-house is a vast weight, and was ill-contrived to lie much on one beam in the middle of the floor. The place being greatly crowded, the beam gave so great a crack as put all the people in a fear. But a second crack set them all on running and crying out at the windows for ladders. I have seen the like before at Dunstan's, Fleet Street, while I was preaching (which occasioned the pulling down and new building of the church),[26] so I reproved them sharply for their fears and would have gone on to preach, but see the strange hand of God on her that set all the work on foot! After the first crack she got down the stairs through the crowd, where others could not get that were stronger. The first man she met, she asked him what profession he was of? He said, a carpenter. Saith she, "Can you suddenly put a prop under the middle of this beam?" The man dwelt close by and had a meet prop ready. He suddenly put it under, while all we above knew nothing of it; but the man's knocking increased the people's fears and cry. We were glad all to be gone, and the next morning took a skilful workman to take up the boards and search the beam, which we saw had two rents, so long and so wide and the sound part left was so slender, that we took it for a wonder that the house fell not suddenly.

But this fright increased my wife's diseased frightfulness; so that she never got off all the effects of it while she lived. The fear and the marvelous deliverance made her promise to God two things: to keep the anniversary memorial of it in public thanksgiving (which she did), and to build a safer place, where they might meet with less fear. And it too deeply touched her mind to think that it was she that took the place and brought them all thither. And if eight hundred persons had been there buried in the ruins, as the Papists were at Blackfriars,[27] O what a dreadful thing it would have been in the heavy loss, the many dolorous families, and the public scandal! These were too great thoughts to fall on a weak and too passionate nature.

According to her promise she paid for that place and presently set to seek and build another. And there was there no fit grounds near it to be had, but two; one of which was in Oxenden Street, which she could not have without giving £30 a year ground rent, and to be at all the charge of building on it, and this but for a lease not very long. But she must do it by promise and desire. She gets a friend to make the bargain, takes the ground, and begs money to build on it a chapel (which tempted us by the ill-advice of a friend to take also the frontage to the street and build two little houses on it, to our great loss, all her own money and many times more being laid out upon them, much against her inclination).

When that chapel was finished, I began and preached there but one day, being to go on the morrow into the country. It unhappily fell out that Secretary Henry Coventry's[28] house was on the back side of it, who resolved that it should not be used by us. The next Lord's Day when I was far off and left my wife at home, she got one Mr. Seddon, a Derbyshire stranger then come to town, to preach there (an humble pious man, what had suffered imprisonment formerly by Cromwell's party for being for the King's Restoration at the rising of Sir George Booth). Secretary Coventry, thinking I would be there, had got three justices with a warrant as for me [i.e., naming me specifically] to have apprehended me and sent me to jail. But it fell on Mr. Seddon. But because the warrant made for me was so altered as to the name that it suited not his case, after some time of imprisonment he had his Habeas Corpus, and by the justice of worthy Judge Hale and other judges was delivered. But he was a tender man, and my wife felt that she was the occasion (which did her no good), and all the burden lay on her to maintain him, to visit and comfort him, to pay the lawyers and discharge all fees; which as I remember cost her £20. And yet we were calumniated as if I (that was twenty miles off) had put another to suffer in my stead.

When she saw that we could not be suffered to preach in that place which upon her promise she had built, she was very glad that Dr. Lloyd[29] and the parishioners accepted of it for their public worship, asking them no more rent than we were to pay for the ground, and the room over a vestry at £5, and asking no advantage for all the money laid out on the building; yet since that time the purchase of the fee-simple [i.e., freehold] of the chapel ground hath cost me £200 more (and the adjoining ground £200 more, to my great loss).

So much was her heart set on the helping the ignorant, untaught poor about St. James' that she set up a school there to teach some poor children to read, and the catechism,[30] freely, and thereby also relieved a poor honest man that taught them, who hath a wife and many children and no other maintenance of his own (Mr. Bruce). And she would have set up more, had she had money. For this she begged awhile of her good friends, but they quickly gave over, and she paid him mostly of her own, five pounds a year till her death. I mention this to move some charitable people to continue it, and to tell them that in the many great out-parishes of London there are multitudes of the children of the poor that spend their time in idleness and in play and are never taught to read, and that there are many good women very poor that would be glad of a small stipend to teach such to read, and the catechism; and so both might have relief and help. And I think charity can scarce be better used, as honest Mr. Gouge hath in

Wales found by experience.[31] And I would such places in London where the tenth or the fourth person in the parish cannot come to church, and many thousands have disused themselves from God's public worship, and breed up their children accordingly, were pitied as well as Wales.

When she saw that she could not use the chapel she built, she presently hired another near (ready built, for gain) in Swallow Street, that the poor people where I had begun (through God's mercy with considerable success) might still be taught. And when I had there a while continued, and then was kept out (by the officers standing at the door with the Justices' warrant many months together), it was her care and act to refer it to many good ministers, to choose one for the place that would be better endured by them that would not endure me; and a faithful, hard-working, self-denying man was chosen who hath there done much good and still doth.

When I was thence driven, it was her choice that I should go quite to Southwark, each Lord's Day, to preach to a congregation of poor people there.

When Dr. Manton's place at Covent Garden was void,[32] it was her desire that I should preach once a day there, because being near, many of the poor of St. James' would come thither, as they did.

She got from her friends also money to help to build another very useful chapel for another amongst a numerous poor people, where still much good is done. And she promoted two or three such more.

She was very impatient of public collections for the ministers or for the rent of the place, because it sounded mercenary and prejudiced the ignorant and covetous, and troubled the poor that had no money, and therefore did the utmost she could with her own purse and her friends to avoid it, knowing that rent must be paid and ministers and their families must have bread (and it is a pity they should be under the cares of want).

She was so far from crossing me in my preaching freely without salary, or gathering a church that would maintain me, or making collections or getting subscriptions, that she would not have endured any such things had I desired it. Though she knew that the laborer was worthy of his hire and that God had ordained that they that preach the gospel should live of the gospel, yet she knew that all must be done to the furtherance of the gospel, and to edifying; and was of Paul's mind, that would rather die than any should make his glorying void and deprive him of that reward. Therefore it was so far from offending her (as it would be with many ministers' wives that were in want, and might have such maintenance as is their due) that I neither conformed nor took any place of gain, that it was as much by her will as my own that for the first nine or ten years of my ejected state I took not so much as any private gift to supply my wants, except ten pounds a year from Sergeant Fountaine,[33] which his importunity and my civility would not permit me to refuse.

And I take it yet for a greater part of her self-denial and charity that, when her own estate proved much too short to maintain her in the exercise of such good works as she was devoted to, she at length refused not to accept with thanks the liberality of others and to live partly on charity, that she might exercise charity to them that could not so easily get it from others as we could do. And accordingly of latter years diverse faithful pious friends (no way related to us or obliged by us) have been so free, kind, and liberal, that I have much ado to forbear here naming them, in expression of their bounty and my thanks. And I must say of her, that once her pride would not have stooped to be so much beholden as to live on the charity of strangers.

When warrants were out (from Sir Thomas Davis)[34] to distrain of [i.e., confiscate and sell] my goods for fines for my preaching, she did without any repining encourage me to undergo the loss and did herself take the trouble of removing and hiding my library awhile (many score books being so lost), and after she encouraged me to give it away, *bona fide*,[35] some to New England, and the most at home to avoid distraining on them. And the danger of imprisonment and of paying a fine of £40 for every sermon was so far from inclining her to hinder or discourage me from any one sermon, that if she did but think I had the least fear, or self-saving by fleshly wisdom, in shrinking from my undertaken office work, it was so great a trouble to her that she could not hide it (who could too much hide many others).

She was exceeding impatient with any Nonconforming minister that shrunk for fear of suffering or that were overquerulous and concerned about their wants or dangers, and would have no man be minister that had not so much self-denial as to lay down all at the feet of Christ and count no cost or suffering too dear to serve him. She greatly hated choosing or using the sacred ministry for wealth, ease, or honor, or any worldly end serving the flesh under the name of serving Christ, and looking to be reverenced and honored in this taking of God's name in vain.

Accordingly, after some years wherein a larger course had been taken, she was against my persuading parents to devote their children to the ministry, that had but good wits and abilities and were not profane; though my success with some did much encourage me to it heretofore. But her sense of the sin and mischief of bad ministers made her persuade all that in that case she had to do with, to take heed of devoting their sons to the ministry till they had good reason to judge them truly godly; and as she would not have pious persons to marry such as were not pious, on pretense of hopes that God would convert them; so much less would she have such hopes that have no promise from God, made a pretext for devoting unsanctified lads to the sacred office. She saw how many, even of good men's children, profaned the ministry and turned to any course that did but serve their worldly interest, so that she was vehemently against committing any to that office that had not, besides good wits and parts, so great a love of God and souls as to come to it with absolute self-denial, resolved to serve Christ at the dearest rates, and to take his acceptance and the winning of souls for their benefice.

She was not willing to entice any into the way of the ministry as a common trade to live by in the world, and would have had two or three reading, writing, and catechizing schools set up instead of one grammar school; and she would not have parents make scholars of bad children nor send them to the universities, lest when they had a little wordy learning they should make themselves ministers, whether their parents would or not; and thus a swarm of such as had been a few years at the university should think a benefice their due, and take the charge of the souls of many, that never knew the worth of one, nor how it must be qualified and guided.

Her expectations of liberality to the poor from others were too high, and her displeasure too great towards them that denied her; whereupon when she saw a worthy person in debt or prison or great want, she would promise to gather them such a sum, and sometimes she was put to pay most of it herself. But a fortnight or month before she died she promised to get £20 toward the relief of one of known name and worth, and could get but £8 and somewhat over of it, and paid all the rest herself.

Her judgment was that we ought to give more or less to every one that asketh, if we have it; and that neighborhood and notice and asking, next to known indigence and great worth, are marks by which to know to whom God would have us give. I thought that besides these, we must exercise prudence in discerning the degrees of need and worth. But she practiced as she thought, and specially to them in prison for debt, and blamed me if I denied anyone.

Alas, I know many poor widows and others who think they have now lost a mother and are left desolate, whom I could wish some that are able would help, instead of the help which they have lost.

She was much more liberal to many of my own poor kindred than I was; but her way was not to maintain them in idleness, but to take children and set them to some trade, or help them by reason of some special aptitudes.

To her own kindred she bare a most tender love; but her care was most to get them to be good and save their souls, and next to settle them well in the world. I had ever been greatly averse to act as a matchmaker, yet she even compelled me (first satisfying my reason) to find a wife for her only brother's son, who, it is said, was worth to him above £20,000. And her sister's children she loved as if they had been her own, especially three daughters.

There are some things charged on her as faults, which I shall mention. That she busied her head so much about churches and works of charity and was not content to live privately and quietly. But this is only just what profane unbelievers say against all zeal and serious godliness: What needs there all this ado? Doth not Paul call some women his helps in the gospel? He that knows what it is to do good and makes it the business of his life in the world, and knows what it is to give account of our stewardship and to be doomed as the unprofitable slothful servant, will know how to answer this accusation.

Another accusation is that she was wasteful and imprudent in leaving me so much debt. To that I answer: Let anyone that reads what went before, consider what she did, and he will not wonder at her debts. It was not to pamper her own body; she used inexpensive clothing, and a far meaner diet for her own person, I think much less than Cornario's and Lessius' proportion.[36]

And she went into no debt but (by mortgage, or otherwise) she gave the creditors good security for.

But I confess she and I differed in this: I thought I was only to give all my income, and not to borrow to give, unless in some public or extraordinary case; she thought otherwise, that while she could give security, she ought to borrow money to relieve the poor, especially the most worthy. Nor did she draw upon us any debt but what there was not only sufficient security for, but also a fair prospect of ourselves having a competency left, had it pleased God to lengthen her life, and I am far from fearing want myself.

But so much for opening the course of her studies, labors, expenses, and indeed her delights.

Eight

Of Her Mental Qualifications and Her Infirmities

[RICHARD CELEBRATES MARGARET'S QUICK INTELLIGENCE; COMPETENCE IN BUSINESS; BRILLIANCE WITH MORAL DILEMMAS; JOY IN THE GOSPEL, IN GOD, IN GODLINESS, AND IN BEING A DESPISED NONCONFORMIST; EXCELLENCE AS A HOMEMAKER; GENTLE PATIENCE WITH PEOPLE OF ALL SORTS; FAITHFULNESS IN CHIDING HER HUSBAND AS NECESSARY; DESIRE FOR FULLEST SPIRITUAL INTIMACY WITH HIM AT ALL TIMES; AND GREAT LOVE FOR HER MOTHER; DESPITE BATTLES WITH NIGHTMARISH FEARS THAT THREATENED HER SANITY.]

I DOUBT NOT BUT SOME OF THESE ACCUSERS WILL SAY, Why open you all this? Were not you the master? And do you not hereby praise yourself, or else confess that she was your governess?

Perhaps love and grief may make me speak more than many will think fit. But though some passion blind the judgment, some doth but suscitate it to duty, and God made it to that end; and I will not be judged by any that never felt the like.

Did not Christ say of Mary's box of ointment, that it should be remembered wherever the gospel was preached? And was it not Judas that said, What need of this waste? And were not the poor's clothing made by Dorcas, showed to move Peter? The poor we have always with us. Do the covetous believe that what we do to his people we do to Christ?

It was not mine that she gave, but her own, that I am now mentioning, and what she procured.

But I am not ashamed to have been much ruled by her prudent love in many things. And you will the less wonder when I have told you what she and I were.

For myself, my constant pains and weakness and ministerial labors forbade me the care of outward things. I had never much known worldly cares. Before I was married I had no need; afterward she took the care on her, and disuse had made it intolerable to me. I feel now more of it than ever I did, when yet I have so little a way to go.

And as for her (I speak the truth), her apprehension of such things was so much quicker and more discerning than mine, that though I was naturally somewhat tenacious of my own conceptions, her reasons and my experience usually told me that she was in the right and knew more than I. She would at the first hearing understand the matter better than I could do by many and long thoughts.

And the excellency of her reason lay not so much in the speculative as the prudential practical part. I must say that in this I never knew her equal. In very hard cases about what was to be done, she would suddenly open all the way what was to be opened, in the things of the family, estate, or any civil business. And to confess the truth, experience acquainted her that I knew less in such things than she, and therefore was willing she should take it all upon her.

Yes, I will say that (which they that believe me to be no liar will wonder at), except in cases that required learning and skill in theological difficulties, she was better at resolving a case of conscience than most divines that ever I knew in all my life. I often put cases to her which she suddenly so resolved as to convince me of some degree of oversight in my own resolution. Insomuch that of late years, I confess, that I was used to put all, save secret cases, to her and hear what she could say. Abundance of difficulties were brought me, some about restitution, some about injuries, some about references, some about vows, some about marriage promises, and many such like; and she would lay all the circumstances presently together, compare them, and give me a more exact resolution than I could do.

As to religion, we were so perfectly of one mind that I know not that she differed from me in any one point or scarce a circumstance, except in the prudential management of what we were agreed in. She was for universal love of all true Christians, and against appropriating the church to a party, and against censoriousness and partiality in religion. She was for acknowledging all that is of God in Conformists and Nonconformists. But she had much more reverence for the elder Conformists than for most of the young ones, who ventured upon things which Dissenters had so much to say against, without weighing or understanding the reasons on both sides, merely following others for worldly ends without a tender fear of sinning. Especially if any young men of her own friends were inclined merely to swim with the stream, without due trial of the case, it greatly displeased her and she thought hardly of them.

She had in her youth been tempted to doubt of the life to come and of the truth of the Scripture. But she was so resolved and settled therein that her confident assurance of it was the life of all her life and practice.

After all the doubts of her sincerity and salvation and all the fears and sadness thereupon, which cast her into melancholy, she so far overcame them all, that for near these nineteen years that I have lived with her, I think I never heard her thrice speak a doubting word of her salvation, but oft of her hopeful persuasions that we should live together in heaven; it being my judgment and constant practice to make those that I teach understand that the gospel is glad tidings of great joy; and that holiness lies especially in delighting in God, his Word and works, and in his joyful praise and hopes of glory, and in longing for and seeking the heavenly Jerusalem, and in living as fruitfully to the church and others as we can do in the world; and that this must be wrought by the most believing apprehensions of God's goodness as equal to his greatness, and of his great love to mankind manifested in our redemption, and by believing the grace and riches of Christ and the comforting office of the Holy Ghost, and studying daily God's promises and mercies and our everlasting joys; and that religion consists in doing God's commanding will and quietly and joyfully trusting in his promising and disposing will; and that fear and sorrow are but to remove impediments and further all this.

And this doctrine by degrees she drunk in and so fully consented to that (though timorousness was her disease) her judgment was quieted and settled therein.

The nature of true religion, holiness, obedience, and all duty to God and man was printed in her conceptions, in so distinct and clear a character as made her endeavors and expectations constantly look at greater exactness than I and such as I could reach. She was very desirous that we should all have lived in a constancy of devotion and a blameless innocency. And in this respect she was the meetest helper that I could have had in the world (that ever I was acquainted with); for I was apt to be over-careless in my speech and too backward to my duty, and she was always endeavoring to bring me to greater wariness and strictness in both. If I spoke rashly or sharply, it offended her; if I behaved (as I was apt) with too much neglect of ceremony or humble compliment to any, she would modestly tell me of it; if my very looks seemed not pleasant, she would have me amend them (which my weak pained state of body undisposed me to do); if I forgot any week to cate-chize my servants and familiarly instruct them personally (besides my ordinary family duties), she was troubled at my remissness. And whereas of late years my declining vitality and diseased heavi-ness and pain made me much more seldom and cold in profitable conference and discourse in my house than I had been when I was younger and had more ease and spirits and natural vigor, she much blamed me and was troubled at it, as a wrong to herself and others; though yet her judgment agreed with mine, that too much and often table talk of the best things doth but tend to dull the com-mon hearers and harden them under it as a customary thing, and that too much good talk may bring it into contempt or make it ineffectual.

And of late years, my constant weakness and pain made me unable to speak much in my ordinary course of duty; and my writ-ings, preachings, and other public duty (which I ever thought I was bound to prefer before lesser) did so wholly take up those few hours of the day which I had out of my bed that I was seldomer in secret prayer with my wife than she desired.

Indeed, it troubleth me to think how oft I told her that I never understood Solomon's words, Ecclesiastes 7:16, but by the exposi-tion of her case—*Be not righteous overmuch, neither make thyself overwise: why shouldst thou destroy thyself?* I doubt not but Solomon spake of humane, civil righteousness and wisdom, as a means respecting temporal prosperity or adversity, rather than spiritual holy righteousness, respecting God's everlasting reward; or if it were extended to religious righteousness, it can be but against superstition, falsely called righteousness.

But as to our present case, I must thus resolve the question, Whether one can be religiously wise and righteous overmuch? And I answer, that we must distinguish 1. material and formal righteousness 2. between objective and subjective measures of it 3. of the good and bad consequents and effects.

And 1. no man can be formally and properly too wise or too righteous. Else it would charge God with error, for formal proper righteousness is nothing but our conformity to God's governing will. And if our obedience were too much, and to be blamed, God's commands were to be blamed that required it. But very strict actions are commonly called righteousness, as a written prayer or words are commonly called prayer, though properly wanting the form,[37] it is not so. And not only a good object, but a right end, principle and mode and circumstances, go to make an action righteous.

2. That action which compared with the object cannot possibly be overwise and righteous, yet as compared with the agent or subject may be too much. No man can know, believe, or love God too much, answerable to his perfections; but one may possibly be transported with so earnest a desire of God, Christ, Christian society, holiness, and heaven as may be more than head and health can bear, and so it may be too much for the subject.

3. Therefore the probable effects must be weighed. He that should meditate, read, yea, love God so intensely as to distract him, would do it overmuch. He that would do a good work precisely, when the exactness would hinder the substance of another, perhaps a better work, would be righteous overmuch. And I thought this the case sometime of my dear wife. She set her head and heart so intensely upon doing good that her head and body would hardly bear it. As holy set [i.e., topical and systematic]

meditation is no duty to a melancholy person that cannot do it without confusion and danger of distraction, so many other duties are no duties when they will do more harm than good. And a man is limited in his capacity and his time. No man can do all the good he would, and to omit a greater for the better doing of a lesser, or to omit the substance of the one for exacter doing of another, I thought was to be unrighteous by being righteous overmuch.

She (and some others) thought I had done better to have written fewer books, and to have done those few better. I thought while I wrote not needlessly, the modal imperfection of two was less evil than the total omission of one. She thought I should have spent more time in religious exercise with her, my family, and my neighbors, though I had written less. I thought there were many to do such work that would not do mine, and that I chose the greatest, which I durst not omit, and could not do both in the measure that I desired else to have done.

As she saith (before cited) herself, that if she was but in a condition in which God's service was costly to her, it would make her know whether she were sincere or not; so she had her wish and proved her sincerity by her costliest obedience. It cost her not only her labor and estate, but somewhat of her trouble of body and mind; for her knife was too keen and cut the sheath. Her desires were more earnestly set on doing good than her tender mind and head could well bear; for indeed her great infirmity was the four passions of love, desire, fear, and trouble of mind. Anger she either had very little next none, or little made it known. She rarely ever spoke in an angry manner. She could not well bear to hear one speak loud or hastily or eagerly or angrily, even to those that deserved it. My temper in this she blamed as too quick and earnest. When her servants did any fault unwillingly, she scarce ever told them of it; when one lost ten pounds' worth of linen in carriage carelessly, and another ten pounds' worth of plate by negligence, she showed no anger at any such thing. If servants had done amiss and we could not prove it or knew not which did it, she would never ask them herself nor suffer others to do so, lest it should tempt them to hide it by a lie (unless it were a servant that feared God and would not lie).

I took her deep and long sense of the faults of over-loved persons to be one of her greatest faults. But no one was ever readier to forgive a fault confessed, or which weakness and religious differences caused. I will give but one instance.

The good woman whom she used to hire the rooms over St. James' Market House was greatly against the Book of Common Prayer, and first made my wife feel whether I meant to use it before she would take it. I told her I intended not to use it but would not promise her. Upon that my wife told her that I would not. After this I caused the reader to read the Psalms, Chapters, Creed, and Decalogue, and I used the Lord's Prayer;[38] and I openly told them that we met not as a separate distinct church, but for the time to supply the notorious necessities of the people and as helpers of the allowed ministry. The good woman thought this had been reading the Common Prayer, and in a letter which I now find, accused my wife with five or six vehement charges for telling her I would not read the Common Prayer. My wife was of my mind for the matter, but greatly offended with me for seeming to do it for the avoiding of danger; and was so far from not pardoning these false, smart accusations that she never once blamed the good woman, but loved her, cared for her, and relieved her in sickness to the death, but hardly forgave me. And yet she discouraged me from attending all other places, if the ministers were not of my mind (by prudent diversity).

Much less did her sufferings from the times distemper her. She hath blamed me for naming in print my losses, imprisonment, and other sufferings by the Bishops as being over-selfish querulousness when I should rather with wonder be thankful for the great mercy we yet enjoyed. Though I think I never mentioned them as over-concerned about the sufferings but as a necessary evincing of the nature of the cause and as part of the necessary history or matter of fact in order to decide it. She as much disliked the silencing of the ministers as any; but she did not love to hear it much complained of, save as the public loss, nor to hear Conformists talked against as a party, nor the faults of the conscientious sort of them aggravated in a siding, factious manner.

But she was prone to over-love her relations and those good people (poor as much as rich) whom she thought the most upright. The love was good, but the degree was too passionate.

She over-earnestly desired their spiritual welfare. If these whom she over-loved had not been as good and done as well as she would have them, in innocent behavior, in piety, and (if rich) in liberality, it over-troubled her, and she could not bear it.

She was apt, when she set her mind and heart upon some good work which she counted great for the welfare of some dear friend, to be too much pleased in her expectations and self-made promises of the success, and then almost overturned with trouble when they disappointed her. And she too impatiently bore unkindnesses from the friends that were most dear to her or whom she had much obliged. Her will was set upon good, but her weakness could not bear the crossing and frustration of it.

But the great infirmity which tyrannized over her was a diseased fearfulness against which she had little more free will or power than a man in an ague or frost against shaking cold. Her nature was prone to it; and I said before, abundance of sad accidents made that, and trouble of mind, her malady. Besides (as she said) four times in danger of death; and the storming of her mother's house by soldiers, firing part, killing, plundering, and threatening the rest; the awakenings of her conversion; the sentence of death by sickness presently, before her peace was settled; the fire next her lodgings in Sweeting's Alley; the burning of a merchant, his wife and family, in Lothbury over against her brother Upton's door; the common terror and confusion at Dunstan's Church in Fleet Street, when they thought the church was falling on their heads while I was preaching, and the people cast themselves down from the galleries; her mother's death; the friendless state she thought she was then left in; the great plague; the burning of London; the crack and danger of her chamber in Aldersgate Street; the crack and confusion at St. James' Market House; the many fires and talk of firing since; the common rumors of murders and massacres; the death and dangers of many of her friends, and my own illness. More than all these concurred to make fear and aptness to be troubled to be her disease, so that she much dreamed of fire and murderers; and her own dreams worked half as dangerously on her as realities, so that she could not bear the clapping of a door or anything that had suddenness, noise, or fierceness in it. But all this was more the malady of her body than of her soul, and I accounted had little moral guilt; and I took it for an evidence of the power of grace that so timorous a person had overcome most of her fears of hell and God's desertion and was more fearless of persecution, imprisonment, or losses and poverty thereby, than I or any that I remember to have known.

And though her spirits were so quick, and she so apt to be

troubled at men's sin whom she much loved, she greatly differed from me in her bearing with them and behavior toward them. My temper and judgment much led me to use my dependents, servants, and friends according to the rules of church discipline; and if they heard not loving, private admonitions once, twice, and thrice, to speak to them more sharply, and then before others, and to turn them off if yet they would not amend. But her way was to oblige them all by the love, kindness, and bounty that she was able, and to bear with them year after year while there was hope, and at last not to desert them but still to use them so as she thought was likest at least to keep them in a state of hope from the badness which expressed displeasure might cause. I could not have borne with a son, I think, as she could do where her kindness was at her own choice; and yet she more disliked the least fault than I did, and was more desirous of their greatest innocency and exactness.

Indeed, she was so much for calmness, deliberation, and doing nothing rashly and in haste, and my condition and business as well as temper made me do and speak much so suddenly, that she principally differed from me and blamed me in this: Every considerable case and business she would have me take time to think much of before I did it or spoke or resolved of anything. I knew the counsel was good for one that could stay, but not for one that must ride post: I thought still I had but a little time to live; I thought some considerable work still called for haste. I have these forty years been constantly conscious of the sin of losing time: I could not spare an hour; I thought I could understand the matters in question as well at a few thoughts as in many days. And yet she (that had less work and more leisure, but a far quicker apprehension than mine) was all for staying to consider, and against haste and eagerness in almost everything, and notwithstanding her over-quick and feeling temper, was all for mildness, calmness, gentleness, pleasingness, and serenity.

She had an earnest desire of the conversion and salvation of her servants and was greatly troubled that so many of them (though tolerable in their work) went away ignorant or strangers to true godliness, as they came; and such as were truly converted with us she loved as children.

One infirmity made her faulty in the omission of her duty. She was wont to say that she had from her childhood imprinted a deep fear and hatred of hypocrisy on her mind, that she could never do the outside of her duty, as to the speaking part, for fear of hypocrisy. I scarce ever met with a person that was abler to speak long, for matter and good language, without repetitions, even about religious things; and few that had more desire that it were well done; and yet she could not do it herself for fear of seeming to be guilty of ostentation. In good company she would speak little of that which she most desired to hear. When I was at any time from home, she would not pray in the family, though she could not endure to be without it. She would privately talk to the servants and read good books to them. Most of the open speaking part of religion she omitted, through a diseased enmity to ostentation and hypocrisy. But of late years, when she saw me and others too sparing in profitable speech to young and ignorant people, she confessed that she saw her error, and that even an hypocrite, using but the words and outside of religion, was better to others than silence and unprofitable omission was.

Her household affairs she ordered with so great skill and decency as that others much praised that which I was no fit judge of. I had been bred among plain, lower-class people, and I thought that so much washing of stairs and rooms, to keep them as clean as their trenchers and dishes, and so much ado about cleanliness and trifles, was a sinful eccentricity and expense of servants' time, who might that while have been reading some good book. But she that was otherwise bred had somewhat other thoughts.

Her great tender impatience lay much in her ears. She could not bear (without great reason) a disputing contradiction, nor yet to hear sad tidings, nor any hard prognostic; and it was because she felt the weakness of her own head, and for twenty years lived in too great fears of the overthrow of her understanding. And I was apt to think it was but a passionate fanciful fear, and was too apt to be impatient with her impatiency and with every trouble of her mind, not enough considering how great tenderness in all her discourse she needed; though I remember nothing else that ever I showed impatience to her in; but ever since her first danger and strong affection, I could hardly bear any signification of her displeasure and discontent. And she was wont oft to say, it is a great mercy of God not to know what will befall us in this world, nor how we shall be sick, or suffer, or die, that our foreknowledge may not anticipate our sorrows, though in the general we should always be ready.

She was the greatest honorer of her mother, and most sincerely loved her, that ever I knew a child do her parent. She believed the promise of the fifth commandment, and believed that it did imply an answerable curse to them that broke it. And that as honoring parents hath even the promise of blessings on earth, so the dishonoring them is like to bring a curse upon the person or family that is guilty of it; and that how great soever their present prosperity may seem, it is coming and will overtake them either in their bodies, children, or estates. Proverbs 30:17, *The eye that mocketh at his father, and despiseth to obey his mother, the ravens of the valley shall pick it out, and the young eagles shall eat it.* And such by Moses' law were to be put to death, Deuteronomy 27:16, *Cursed be he that setteth light by his father or his mother; and let all the people say Amen.* And will God suspend it till the sinner saith, Amen? Oh no. And what is that person's case that liveth under this curse of God? If the body escape it, and posterity escape it, and the estate escape it, yea, and a seared conscience escape it a few years, the soul will not escape it forever without deep and thorough repentance, for Christ hath redeemed none but sincere penitents from the curse; yea, even such seldom escape the temporal sharp chastisement.

And very worthy was her mother of her love and honor. All her letters to her when she was from home I find now laid up by her as a treasure. I will transcribe one of them, that you may perceive her plain and honest care of her children's souls.

In 1659, she writes thus:

My dear child,

My greatest trouble is that I can have no better account of your health of body, yet surely the cure of the soul is of far more worth. Therefore I faint not, else I should not submit under the heavy stroke which I have justly deserved. Who knows but my sins may be some cause of thy distress of soul? However let us return to the Lord, and he will heal all our breaches, and will bind up all our sores, and will give us a house not made with hands, eternal in the heavens; here we shall never be forced asunder, and all infirmities shall be left behind; and we shall take up all pleasure in the enjoyment of our heavenly Redeemer. In the meantime let us with courage and patience and confidence press hard toward the mark, for the prize of that calling which was set before us. For the things which are seen are temporal, but the things which are not seen are eternal. I can go no further, but cannot forget to be

Thy truly loving mother,
M[ary]. H[anmer].

This was written to her [i.e., Margaret] in her sickness, when, for better air, she lay at old Mr. Richard Foley's house at Stourbridge.[39]

I have transcribed this to show the mind and care of the good gentlewoman, and what cause I and my neighbors had of compassion to her in her sorrows when she was separated from an only son, whose welfare she had prosecuted with so strong affection and long labor and patience,[40] and began to have much comfort in this daughter whom she had formerly least valued, and thought she must so suddenly leave her.

I will add that, though because for nineteen years I was so seldom from her, she had few letters of mine, yet those papers which she had I find now among her reserved papers. And that you may see what it was that I thought she most desired, and what she herself most valued, I will here add one of them (not venturing to trouble such with more, as are affected little with any matters but their own, which is the case of most). I reproduce this rather than others, partly also as an act of repentance for those failings of her just expectations by the neglect of such helps as I should have given her, which I had here mentioned. For though she oft said that before she married me she expected more sourness and unsuitableness than she found; yet I am sure that she found less zeal and holiness and strictness in all words and looks and duties, and less help for her soul, than she expected. And her temper was to aggravate a fault much more in her nearest and dearest friends than in any others, and to be far more troubled at them. But this use [i.e., applicatory inference] she made of my too cold and care-less converse and of all my impatiency with her impatience, and of all my hasty words, that she had long thought she had no grace because she reached not higher than almost any reach on earth, and because she had many passions and infirmities perceived by me and many other esteemed teachers, that were all as bad as she; and now she saw that grace doth stand with more faultiness than she had imagined, and that all our teaching much excelled the frame of our souls and lives, and was much more worthy to be followed; and therefore that God would also pardon such failings as her own.

Though I have received none from you but one by Mr. H., I will not be avenged on you by the like. I have nothing of news or business to communicate but to tell you that we are all yet as well as you left us, excepting what your absence causeth. And yet I must confess that I find it is easier to be oft speaking to God when I have nobody else to speak to, than when there are other competitors, expectants, or inter-polators. Just as I can easier now fill my paper to thee with some speech of God, when I have nothing else to put into it, than I can when many other matters are craving every one a place. It is our shame that the love and glory of God doth not silence every other suitor, and even in the midst of crowds and business take us up and press every creature and occasion for their service. But while we are weak and com-passed with flesh, we must not only consider what we should do but what we can do. It is our great fault that we are no skilfuller and faithfuller in helping one another, that we might miss each other on better reasons than merely from the inclinations of love. I hope God will make us better hereafter, that when we are asunder each of us may say, I miss the help for watchfulness and heavenliness, for true love and thankfulness to God, which I was wont to have. But O! what an enemy is a naughty heart! which maketh us unable for our duty alone, and makes us need the help of others, and yet will not suffer us to use it when we have it. When we are alone it maketh us impediments to ourselves, and when we are in company it maketh us impediments to others. Yet there is none, no, not the weakest of Christians, but there is much in them that we might improve. But we are so bad and backward at it, that Satan too commonly hath his end in making us unprofitable to each other. If a good horse or a good house be a valuable mercy, how much more is a good friend? But art and industry are necessary to the improvement. And no wonder when we fetch not the help and comfort which we might have from God, from Christ himself, from heaven, from Scripture, for want of improving skill and industry. O how easy it is, when our friends are taken from us, to say: Thus I might and should have used them, rather than so to use them while we have them. I hope God will help me to make some better use of thee while we are together and at a distance. O let not a hearty request to God for each other be any day wanting! Dear heart, the time of our mutual help is short (O let us use it accordingly); but the time of our reaping the fruit of this and all holy endeavors and preparatory mercies will be endless. Yet a little while and we shall both be with Christ. He is willing of us, and I hope we are willing of him and of his grace, though the flesh be weak. I am absent, but God is still with you, your daily Guide and Keeper; and I hope you will labor to make him your daily comfort. And now you have none to divert and hinder you, to say: *When I awake I am still with thee.* And when you are up: *I have set the Lord always before me; because he is at my right hand, I shall not be moved.* And when thoughts crowd in: *In the multitude of my thoughts within me, thy comforts delight my soul.* And when thoughts would trouble and perplex you: *My meditation of him shall be sweet, and I will delight in the Lord.* And when your wants and duty call you to him: *It is good for me to draw nigh to God.*

All other comforts will be, as the things are which we take comfort in; that is, helpful if the things be helpful and used but as helps, hurtful if the things be hurtful or hurtfully used, vain if the things be vain, short if the things be transitory, and durable if the things are durable to us. And this is the chief comfort which you and I must have in one another, that is, as helpful toward God, and as our converse with him will be durable. The Lord forgive my great unprofitableness and the sin that brought me under any disabilities to answer your earnest and honest desires of greater helps than I afford you, and help me yet to amend it toward you. But though my soul be faulty and my strength of nature fail, be sure that he will be a thousandfold better to thee, even here, than such crooked, feeble, useless things, as is

Thy R.B.
From Hampden.[41]

Nine

Of Her Bodily Infirmities and Her Death

[RICHARD BLENDS PASTORAL AND MEDICAL OBJECTIVITY WITH
RESTRAINED PERSONAL HEARTACHE AS HE TELLS OF
MARGARET'S LAST ILLNESS AND DEATH.]

HER DISEASED FEARFULNESS and many former sicknesses I have
mentioned before. A great pain of the head held her from her
youth, two or three days every fortnight, or little more; and upon
everything that did irritate the matter she had a constant constriction in the lungs, a great incapacity of much exercise, motion, or
any heating thing. Ever since her sickness, 1659, she hath lived in
an unwarranted fear of insanity, which greatly hurt her. It was
because she had an aunt long so, deceased, and her parents were
naturally passionate, and her spirits over-quick, and her blood thin
and mobile, and though wisdom hid it from others in her converse, she felt the trouble of her own mind in things, as aforesaid,
that much displeased her; and so lived in a constant fear, which
tended to have brought on her what she feared. But her understanding was so far from failing that it was higher and clearer than
other people's, but, like the treble strings of a lute, strained up to
the highest, sweet, but in continual danger.

About three years ago, by the mispersuasion of a friend, drink-
ing against the colic a spoonful of powdered ginger every morning
near a quarter of a year together, and then falling into some over-
whelming thoughts besides, it overthrew her head for a few days;
but God, in great mercy, soon restored her.

Ever since that time her headache abated, and she complained of pain in one of her breasts, and her uncurable timorousness settled her in a mental condition that she should have a cancer (which I saw no cause to fear); but she could neither endure to hear that it was none, or that it was; but in fearing uncertainty, prepared constantly for a sad death. And several friends, neighbors, and relations lately dying of cancers increased her fear, but she seemed to be prepared cheerfully to undergo it.

The many and weekly rumors of plots, firings, and massacres, etc.,[42] much increased this fear, as is aforesaid; and the death of very many neighbors, young, strong, and excellent Christians, of greatest use and many near friends, did greatly add to her sadness and expectations of death. But little of this was seen to any; she purposely carried it pleasantly, and as merrily to others, when she was troubled.

The fears of a cancer made her take the waters for physic often, and she kept down her body so in her diet, that about five ounces of milk, or milk and water, with a little chocolate in it, morning and night, and about one or two bits [i.e., pieces of meat] at dinner was her diet for many years.

At last, about ten weeks before her sickness, almost all her pain went out of her breast, and all fixed in a constant pain upon the right kidney. She for several days drank Barnet waters; but I think they were the final contributing cause of her sickness, along with too much tincture of amber, which worked too powerfully on her brain and suddenly cast her into strong disturbance and delirium, in which, though the physicians, with great kindness and care, did omit nothing in their power, she died the twelfth day. She fell sick on Friday, June 3, 1681, and died June 14.

Though her understanding never perfectly returned, she had a very strong remembrance of the affecting passages of her life, from her childhood. Mrs. Corbet (whom she dearly loved, and had newly got into the house to be her companion), with others, standing by, she cried out to me, "My mother is in heaven, and Mr. Corbet is in heaven, and thou and I shall be in heaven." And even in her last weakness she was persuaded of her salvation.

She oft showed us that her soul did work toward God, crying out (complaining of her head): "Lord, make me to know what I have done for which I undergo all this. Lord, I submit; God chooseth best for me." She desired me to pray by her, and seemed quietly to join to the end. She heard diverse psalms, and a chapter read, and repeated part, and sung part of a psalm herself. The last words that she spoke were: "My God, help me! Lord, have mercy upon me!"

God had been so many years training her up under the expectation and preparations for death, as made the case of her soul less grievous to me, as no way doubting of her salvation; and knowing that a distracting fever or frenzy, or an inflammation or disturbance of the animal spirits or brain, or an abscess may befall the best as soon as the worst. I thank God that she was never under any melancholy which tempted her to any of those doleful evils, which many score, I think, that have been with me (of several ways of education) have been sadly tempted to.[43] She near nineteen years lived with me, cheerful, wise, and a very useful life, in constant love and peace and concord, except our differing opinions about trivial occurrences, or our disputing or differing mode of talk.

She was buried on June 17 in Christ's Church, in the ruins, in her own mother's grave. The grave was the highest next the old altar, or table, in the chancel, on which this her daughter had caused a very fair, rich, large marble stone to be laid, Anno 1661, about twenty years ago; on which I caused to be written her titles and some Latin verses and these English ones:

> Thus must thy flesh to silent dust descend,
> Thy mirth and worldly pleasure thus will end:
> Then happy, holy souls but woe to those
> Who heaven forgot, and earthly pleasures chose:
> Hear now this preaching grave without delay,
> Believe, repent, and work while it is day.

But Christ's church on earth is liable to those dangers of which the Jerusalem above is in no danger. In the doleful flames of London, 1666, the fall of the church broke this great marble all to pieces, and it proved no lasting monument: and I hope this paper monument erected by one that is following even at the door, in some passion indeed of love and grief, but in sincerity of truth, will be more publicly useful and durable than that marble stone was.

Ten

Some Uses Proposed to the Reader from This History, as the Reasons Why I Wrote It

[RICHARD EXPLAINS HOW HIS NARRATIVE CONFIRMS THE
REALITY OF THE REGENERATING WORK OF GRACE AND THE
TRUTH OF THE SCRIPTURES THAT DESCRIBE IT, AND DRAWS
FROM THE STORY ALL SORTS OF LESSONS ABOUT CONVERSION
AND THE CHRISTIAN LIFE AND THE BURDENS THAT ACCOMP-
ANY THE BLESSINGS OF MARRIAGE.]

IF THIS NARRATIVE BE USELESS TO THE READERS, it must needs be
the sin of the author, for idle writing is worse than idle words; but
I think it useful (with that which followeth) to all these ends to
considering men.

It may help to convince those that are inclined to Sadducism, or
infidelity, and believe not the testimony of the sanctifying Spirit as
to the truth of the Word of God; but take holiness, as it differs
from heathen morality, to be but fancy, hypocrisy, custom, or self-
conceit. A man that never felt the working of God's special grace
in his own heart is hardly brought to believe that others have that
which he never had himself. And this turneth usually to diabolical
malignity, inclining them to hate those, and revile or despise them
as deluded, proud, fanatic hypocrites, who pretend to be any better than they are or to have that which they take to be but a conceit. All their religious thoughts they take for the dreams of crazed
or proud persons; and their holy discourse and prayers, but for
canting and vain babbling. But acquaintance, if intimate with gracious persons, might convince them of their moral error; and true

history methinks may do much toward it.

I confess, with thanks to God, that having these forty years found that all our holiness and comfort depends upon our certain persuasion of the life of retribution following, and that our certainty of this depends upon our certain belief of the Holy Scriptures; and we being here in the dark, and too apt to doubt of all that we see not, there are several first-hand experiences or present certainties which have been a great succor to my faith, to save me from temptations to unbelief and doubting and confirm my assurance that the Scripture is God's Word.

1. In that I undoubtedly see and hear that through all the world there is just such depravity in human nature as the Scripture describeth for [i.e., as constituting] original sin; which condition cannot be the state of man's integrity, when his reason is much convinced of much of the duty to God, man, and himself which he will not do, and of most of the great sins which he will not forsake.

2. I see the Scripture clearly verified in mentioning the common enmity and war between the serpent's and the holy seed; it is notorious through the world, in all ages and countries, an enmity which no relation or interest reconcileth.

3. I feel and see the Scripture verified, which describeth all the temptations of Satan, and the secret war within us between the spirit and the flesh.

4. And I feel and see the Scripture fulfilled, which promiseth a blessing on God's Word and his ordinances.

5. And I feel and see the Scripture fulfilled, which describeth the renewing work of the Holy Ghost and the spiritual difference of the sanctified from others. This is not only in myself, but in

others (O how many hundred holy persons have I known) the witness of Christ's truth and power; and is as Joshua's and Caleb's bunch of grapes to assure me of the land of promise and God's truth, which I see fulfilled in them. Can I doubt of holiness when I feel it and see it in the effects?

6. Even as it persuadeth me the easilier to believe that there are devils, when I see their very nature and works in devils incarnate, and see what a kingdom Satan plainly ruleth in the world; and to believe that there is a hell when I see so much of hell on earth.

It may teach us that the state of godliness is not to be judged of by the fears and sorrows in which it usually begins. A man's life is not like his infancy at his birth. The fears and penitent sorrows, which foolishly fleshly sinners fly from, do tend to everlasting peace and joy; and perfect love will cast out all tormenting fears, unless it be those of a timorous diseased temper which have more of sickness than of sin and will be laid aside with the body, which was their cause. A life of peace and joy on earth may succeed the tremblings of the newborn convert; but a life of full everlasting joy will certainly succeed the perseverance and victory of every believing holy soul.

It may warn all to take heed of expecting too much from so frail and bad a thing as man. My dear wife did look for more good in me than she found, especially lately in my weakness and decay. We are all like pictures that must not be looked on too near. They that come near us find more faults and badness in us than others at a distance know.

It should greatly warn us to take notice of small beginnings; even a spark of affection, honest in the kind, may kindle a flame not easily quenched. How great a matter may a little fire kindle!

Almost all sin beginneth in a seed or spark which is very hardly known to be a sin or danger.

Yea, it should warn all to keep all the thoughts, affections, and passions under a constant watch and obedience to God, and know first whether God command them and allow them.

And this history may teach us that, though God usually begin (as is said) our conversion in fears and penitent sorrows, it is holy and heavenly joy which it tendeth to, as more desirable; and we should chiefly seek and should labor to moderate fear and sorrow, and not think we can never have enough. It is too common an error with honest souls to think that a hard heart lieth most in want of sorrow and tears, when as it lieth most in want of a tractable compliance and yielding to the commands and will of God, and in an iron neck and obstinate disobedience to God; and to think that a new and tender heart is principally a heart that can weep and mourn, when it is chiefly a heart that easily receiveth all the impressions of God's commands and promises and threats, and easily yieldeth to his known will.

And this may greatly warn us to fear and avoid self-willedness; I mean a will of our own that runs before the will of God and is too much set on anything which God hath not promised; and knows not how to bear frustration or denial, but saith as Rachel: *Give it me, or I die.* We must learn to follow and not to lead, and to say: *The will of the Lord be done; not mine, Lord, but thine;* and in every estate to be content. There is no rest but in God's will.

Yet this tells us that God dealeth better with his weak servants than they deserve, and turneth that oft time to their good, which they deserved should have been their greatest suffering.

This history (and my great experience) saith that *there is a friend that sticketh closer than a brother,* Proverbs 18:24; and that it was God's Spirit that said, Proverbs 27:10: *Thy own friend, and thy father's friend forsake not; neither go into thy brother's house in the day of thy calamity: for better is a neighbor that is near than a brother that is far off.*

This history tells us how great a mercy it is to have a body meet to serve the soul, and how great an affliction to have an unruly inclination from the body's temper; and what a tyrant excessive fear is, and how great a blessing it is to have such a passion as faith can rule, and easily quiet.

It tells you also how manifold temptations and affliction God's servants are liable to in this life.

And it tells you that our greatest good or evil is nearest us. Next God, the best is in our souls, and there is the worst; and next in our bodies, and next in our nearest friends. And it may teach all to expect their greatest sorrows from those or that which they most excessively love, and from whom they have the highest expectations. Only God cannot be loved more than he deserveth. Sorrow beginneth in inordinate love to and joy in what is good.

And it tells us that God's service lieth more in deeds than in words. My dear wife was faulty indeed in talking so little of religion in company (except it were unresistable to confute in few words an opposer or reviler of religion). But her religion lay in doing more than talk. Yet her example tells us that it is one of Satan's wiles to draw us to one sin to avoid another, and to make us think that nothing is a duty that hath great inconveniences, or which we can foresee some men will receive hurt from; and so to be unrighteous by being righteous overmuch, and leave much undone for fear of doing it amiss; by which rule we should scarce ever do anything that God commands. *He that observeth the winds shall not sow, and he that regardeth the clouds shall not reap,* Ecclesiastes 11:4. I speak this on her (at last confessed) error of omitting reasonable speech and duty for fear of hypocrisy and ostentation (which my great friend, Judge Hale,[44] was just so guilty of, as I know, and the writers of his *Life* confess; he would make no great show of zeal in religion lest, if he did anything amiss, religion should be reproached for his sake). Cardinal Richelieu was wont to say (as is written of him) that he hated no counselor more than those that were always saying: *Let us do it better,* by that hindering the doing of much at all.

You see here, that suitableness in religious judgment and disposition preserveth faster love and concord (as it did with us) than suitableness in age, education, and wealth; but yet those should not be imprudently neglected. Nothing causeth so near and fast and comfortable an union as to be united in one God, one Christ, one Spirit, one church, one hope of heavenly glory; yet accidental unsuitableness should be avoided as far as may be.

There are some great men who know their own names, who (as I have most credible information) have, to greater than themselves, represented me not only as covetous, but as mutable for my marriage.

To whom I now give this satisfaction. As to covetousness, my vindication is a matter unfit for the ears of the world, if reverend men's backbitings (the same that troubles our common peace) did not make it partly necessary. Through God's mercy and her prudent care, I lived in plenty, and so do still, though not without being greatly beholden to diverse friends, and I am not poorer than when I married; but it is not by marriage, nor by anything that was hers before. As to my mutability: Whereas one of them reports that I said unto him that I thought the marriage of ministers had so great inconveniences that, though necessity made it lawful, yet it was but lawful, that is, to be avoided as far as lawfully we may; I answer that I did say so to him, and I have never changed my judgment. Yea, my wife lived and died in the same mind. And I here freely advise all ministers that have not some kind of necessity to think of these few reasons among many:

1. The work of the sacred ministry is enough to take up the whole man, if he had the strength and abilities of many men. O how much there is to do oftentimes with one ignorant or scandalous or sad despairing soul! And who is sufficient for all that is to be done to hundreds or thousands! In the primitive church every congregation had many ministers; but covetousness of clergy and people will now allow scarce two to very great parishes. I did not marry till I was silenced and ejected and had no flock or pastoral cure. Believe it, he that will have a wife must spend much of his time in her conference, prayer, and other family duties, with her. And if he have children, O how much care, time, and labor they will require! I know it, though I have none. And he that hath servants must spend time in teaching them and in other duties for them, besides the time and perhaps caring thoughts that all his family expenses will require. And then it will disquiet a man's mind to think that he must neglect his family or his flock and hath undertaken more than he can do. My conscience hath forced me many times to omit secret prayer with my wife when she desired it, for want of time, not daring to omit far greater work.

2. And a minister can scarce look to win much influence on his flock if he be not able to oblige them by gifts of charity and liberality. And a married man hath seldom anything to spare; especially if he have children that must be provided for, all will seem too little for them. Or if he have none, housekeeping is chargeable, when a single man may have entertainment at easy rates; and most women

are weak and apt to live in fear of want, if not in covetousness; and have many wants real or fancied of theirs to be supplied.

3. In a word, St. Paul's words are plain to others, but concern ministers much more than other men. First Corinthians 7:7, etc., *I would that all men were as I myself. It is good for them that they abide even as I. 28, Such shall have trouble in the flesh. 32, I would have you without carefulness. He that is unmarried careth for the things that belong to the Lord, how he may please the Lord: but he that is married careth for the things of the world, how he may please his wife.* This is true. And believe it, both caring for the things of the world and caring to please one another are businesses and troublesome businesses; care for house-rent, for children, for servants' wages, for food and raiment, but above all for debts, are very troublesome things; and if cares choke the Word in hearers, they will be very unfit for the mind of a student and a man that should constantly dwell on holy things.

And the pleasing of a wife is usually no easy task. There is an unsuitableness in the best and wisest and most alike. Faces are not so unlike as the apprehensions of the mind. They that agree in religion, in love and interest, yet may have different apprehensions about occasional occurrences, persons, things, words, etc. That will seem the best way to one that seems the worst to the other. And passions are apt to succeed and serve these differences. Very good people are hard to be pleased. My own dear wife had high desires of my doing and speaking better than I did, but my badness made it hard for me to do better. But this was my benefit; for it was but to put me on to be better, as God himself will be pleased. That it is hard to please God and holy persons is only our fault. But there are too many that will not be pleased unless you will contribute to their sin, their pride, their wastefulness, their superfluities and childish fancies, their covetousness and passions; and too many who have such passions that it requireth greater skill to please them than almost any that the wisest can attain. And the discontents and displeasures of one that is so near you will be as thorns and nettles in your bed.

And Paul concludeth to be unmarried is the better, that we may attend the Lord without distraction, vv. 35, 38.

And what need we more than Christ's own words, Matthew 19:10-12. When they said then: *It is not good to marry,* he answers: *All men cannot receive this saying, save they to whom it is given. For there are some eunuchs who were so born from their mother's womb; and there are some eunuchs who were made eunuchs by men; and there be eunuchs which have made themselves eunuchs for the kingdom of heaven's sake. He that is able to receive it let him receive it.*

O how many sad and careful hours might many a minister have prevented? And how much more good he might have done if (being under no necessity) he had been sooner wise in this?

Another use of this history is to show men that it is not God's or our enemies' afflicting us in worldly losses or sufferings (especially when we suffer for righteousness' sake) which is half so painful as our own inward infirmities. A man's spirit can bear his infirmities of outward crosses, but a wounded spirit who can bear? My poor wife made nothing of prisons, distrainings, reproaches, and such crosses, but her burden was most inward, from her own tenderness, and next from those whom she over-loved. And for mine own part, all that ever either enemies or friends have done against me is but a flea-biting to me in comparison of the daily burden of a pained body and the weakness of my soul in faith, hope, love, and heavenly desires and delights.

And here you may see how necessary patience is and to have a mind fortified beforehand against all sorts of sufferings, that in our patience we may possess our souls. And that the dearest friends must expect to find much in one another that must be borne with, and exercise our patience. We are all imperfect. It hath made me many a time wonder at the prelates that can think it is the way to concord of millions, to force them to consent to all their impositions, even of words and promises and ceremonies, and that in things where conscience must be cautious; whereas even husband and wife, master and servants, have almost daily differences in judging of their common affairs.

And by this history you may see how little cause we have to be over-serious about any worldly matters, and to mind and do them with too much intenseness of affection, and how necessary it is to possess them as if we possessed them not, seeing the time is short and the fashion of this world passeth away. And how reasonable it is that, if we love God ourselves, yea, or our friends, we should long to be with Christ, where they are far more amiable than here, and where in the City of God, the Jerusalem above, we shall delightfully dwell with them for ever; whereas here we were always sure to stay with them but a little while. And had we here known Christ after the flesh, we should so know him no more: whereas believing that we shall soon be with him, even those that never saw him may rejoice with joy unspeakable and full of glory.

Lastly, here you may see that, as God's servants have not their portion or good things in this life, so they may have the same sicknesses and manner of death as others. Lazarus may lie and die in his sores among the dogs at the door, when Dives may have a pompous life and funeral. There is no judging of a man's sincerity or of his future state by his disease or by his diseased death-bed words. He that liveth to God shall die safely into the hand of God, though a fever or delirium hinder him from knowing this, till experience and sudden possession of heaven convince him. *Blessed are the dead that die in the Lord, from henceforth: yea, saith the Spirit, that they may rest from their labors, and their works do follow them* (Revelation 14:13). Therefore in our greatest straits and sufferings, let us comfort one another with these words: *That we shall for ever be with the Lord.* Had I been to possess the company of my friends in this life only, how short would our comfortable converse have been! But now I shall live with them in the heavenly city of God forever. And they, being there of the same mind with my forgiving God and Savior, will forgive all my failings, neglects, and injuries, as God forgiveth them and me. The Lord gave, and the Lord hath taken away; and he hath taken away but that upon my desert, which he had given me undeservedly near nineteen years. Blessed be the name of the Lord. I am waiting to be next. The door is open. Death will quickly draw the veil and make us see how near we were to God and one another, and did not sufficiently know it. Farewell vain world, and welcome true everlasting life.

Finis

Appendix

Two Poems from Poetical Fragments (1681)

1. The Prayer of the Sick, in a Case like Hezekiah's (pp. 75-80) (selected verses)

Eternal God, whose name is Love;
> Whose mercy is my hope and stay:
O hear and help me from above,
> That in distress to thee do pray.
Ashamed to lift up my face,
> Hence from the dust to thee I cry:
Though I have sinned against thy grace,
> Yet unto it alone I fly.

I was at first in sin conceived,
> Then lived a vain and sinful life:
Rebellious flesh which I received
> Is still against thy grace in strife.
Long it was, Lord, alas too long
> Before I knew myself or thee:
Vanity ruled my heart and tongue,
> And O that yet [i.e., now] my soul were free!

But while I sinned thou wast kind,
> And sent'st thy Word and Spirit of grace;
Thy light did change my darkened mind,
> And shewed to me my wretched case.

Though I drew back, thou didst prevail;
    And I gave up myself to thee.
Thou undertook'st for wind and sail;
    Both ship and pilot thou would'st be.

I turned my back on worldly toys,
    And set my face towards glory's shore,
Where thou hast promised highest joys
    And blessedness for evermore.
I took my leave of sin and earth;
    What I had loved, I now did hate;
Ashamed of my former birth,
    I gave my life a newer date.

But since that time how I am tossed,
    Afraid of every storm and wave;
Almost concluding I am lost,
    As if thou would'st not help and save.
If I look out beyond thine Ark,
    Nothing but raging seas I see:
On this side heaven all's deep and dark,
    But I look further unto thee.

Censures and scorns and frowns I bear:
    Storms which before I never found;
And yet all these I should not fear,
    If all at home were safe and sound.
But thy displeasure wounds my heart:
    I have but two parts, flesh and soul:
Both of thy wrath do bear their part,
    And thou hast left me neither whole....

Spare, Lord, and pity thy poor dust,
  That fled into thy ark for peace!
O cause my soul on thee to trust!
  And do not my distress increase.
O keep up life and peace within!
  If I must feel thy chastening rod,
Yet kill not me, but kill my sin,
  And let me know, thou art *my God*....

Pity this poor unworthy soul,
  That here devotes itself to thee:
Resolve my doubts; my fears control;
  And let me thy salvation see.
O let that love which gave me groans
  And taught my needy soul to pray,
Remove my fears, and hear the moans
  Which sorrow breathes forth night and day.

Why art thou, fainting soul, cast down,
  And thus disquieted with fears?
Art thou not passing to thy crown,
  Through storms of pain, and floods of tears?
Fear not, O thou of little faith!
  Art thou not in thy Savior's hand?
Remember what his promise saith:
  Life and death are at his command....

Lord, let me not my covenant break;
  Once I did all to thee resign:

Only the words of comfort speak,
       And tell my soul that *I am thine*.
It's no death when souls hence depart,
       If thou depart not from the soul:
Fill with thy love my fainting heart,
       And I'll not fading flesh condole
       [i.e., sorrow with]….

My God, my love, my hope, my life!
       Shall I be loth to see thy face?
As if this world of sin and strife
       Were for my soul a better place?
O give my soul some sweet foretaste
       Of that which I shall shortly see!
Let faith and love cry to the last,
       Come, Lord, I trust myself with thee.

John 11:14 [and 15] or 16
O let not unbelieving Thomas' words
Be now my answer: but my dearest Lord's. Amen.

2. The Covenant and Confidence of Faith (pp.81-83) (selected verses)

> My whole though broken heart, O Lord,
>> From henceforth shall be thine;
> And here I do my vow record:
>> This hand, these words are mine.
> All that I have, without reserve,
>> I offer here to thee;
> Thy will and honor all shall serve
>> That thou bestow'dst on me.
>
> All that exceptions save I lose;
>> All that I lose I save:
> The treasure of thy love I choose,
>> And thou art all I crave.
> My God, thou hast my heart and hand;
>> I all to thee resign.
> I'll ever to this covenant stand,
>> Though flesh hereat repine.
>
> I know that thou wast willing first,
>> And then mad'st me consent;
> Having thus loved me at the worst,
>> Thou wilt not now repent.
> Now I have quit all self-pretence,
>> Take charge of what's thine own!
> My life, my health, and my defence,
>> Now lie on thee alone.

Now it belongs not to my care
    Whether I die or live:
To love and serve thee is my share,
    And this thy grace must give.
If life be long, I will be glad
    That I may long obey:
If short, yet why should I be sad,
    That shall have the same pay?…

Christ leads me through no darker rooms
    Than he went through before;
He that into God's kingdom comes
    Must enter by this door.
Come, Lord, when grace hath made me meet
    Thy blessed face to see;
For if thy work on earth be sweet,
    What will thy glory be?

Then I shall end my sad complaints
    And weary sinful days,
And join with the triumphant saints
    That sing Jehovah's praise.
My knowledge of that life is small;
    The eye of faith is dim:
But it's enough that Christ knows all,
    And I shall be with him.

This covenant my dear wife in her former sickness
subscribed with a cheerful mind.

JOHN 12:26

Part Three

Great Sadness:
Richard Without Margaret

The Grieving Process

LAURA BINKLEY, LIKE HER SAVIOR, was 33 when she died. A missionary, she was murdered in Moscow in October 1993. She saw it coming, and in her last phone call to her mother said, "Mom, if something happens to me, grieve for me properly."[1]

What does it mean to grieve *properly* when one has lost a daughter, a son, a close companion, or the spouse who was one's own best friend?

Grief at the loss of a loved one is as old as the human race. Everyone who loves will experience it sooner or later, and the greater the love the greater the grief when the time of loss arrives. The message of the booklet title *Christians Grieve Too*[2] needs no underlining: We know that Christ's people leave this world for a better one, yet the pain of grief strikes us down as it does others. When bereaved, says St. Paul (1 Thess. 4:13), we are not to grieve as people without hope would grieve; but strong as our hope may be, grief cannot be avoided. As the enjoyment of another's love invigorates one inside, so the blow of losing someone near and dear drains strength from both mind and body for months and perhaps years. And if the bereavement was unanticipated and not prepared for, grief hits harder and hurts more.

Grief is regularly more draining and harrowing than we thought it could be. As a feeling, it is not unique in that regard: all of us are sometimes overwhelmed—stunned, frightened, devastated, transported—by the intensity of our feelings of surprise, pain, fear, love, and joy. We did not know we could feel so strongly, and words fail us to express our feelings adequately.

A master pianist, asked what he meant by great music, replied: "Music better than can be played." Exactly! The notes have in them more of beauty, power, and what jazzmen call *soul* than any performer ever manages to bring out, and all playings of them leave the players feeling that they have not done justice to what is there. All our attempts to put grief into words seem to us similarly inadequate. At the very time when grief and our verbalizings of it bring us to tears, we find ourselves feeling that our grief is really too deep for tears and too agonizing for words. As we struggle with the ache of loss, the grip of our grief imposes a kind of relational paralysis. It hurts like hell, we say; perhaps it is a true reflection of hell, where the ache of losing God and all good, including the good of community, will be endless; be that as it may, a most painful part of the pain of grief is the sense that no one, however sympathetic and supportive in intention, can share what we are feeling, and it would be a betrayal of our love for the lost one to pretend otherwise. So we grieve alone, and the agony is unbelievable.

In Shakespeare's *King Lear* there is a truly terrible moment when the old king, having learned in the hardest possible way that Cordelia was the only daughter who loved him, carries her corpse onto the stage and calls the company to grieve with him.

Howl, howl, howl, howl! O! you are men of stones:
Had I your tongues and ears, I'd use them so
That heaven's vaults should crack. She's gone for ever.

No actor ever does justice to that dreadful yelling groan or catches the full pathos of Lear's gigantic agony. Shakespeare has given Lear words expressing a depth of desolation "better than can be played"; all attempts to speak the lines seem inadequate to what is there. And the pain racking Lear, as we see, is not simply grief at an insupportable loss, but also a sense of being totally isolated, since none of those around can know and share what he feels; which is how it really is in real life. "I miss her terribly" (I quote from a letter just received)—how many bereaved spouses and parents have used such words, knowing as they did so that they were voicing an essentially private pain into which outsiders could not enter. The loneliness of grief is one of the worst and most draining things about it—and, be it said, one of the most dangerous, too.

Richard, who had a way with words, stated that his memoir of Margaret was "written ... under the power of melting grief." *Melting* pinpoints perfectly the effect of being grief-stricken. The capacity for initiative and enterprise melts—dissolves—away, and so does the power of empathy with and response to others. A half-numb apathy, frequently alternating with bouts of tears, sets in. The first paragraph of *A Grief Observed*, which like the Breviate was written within a month of bereavement, describes grief as feeling like fear ("the same fluttering in the stomach, the same restlessness, the yawning. I keep on swallowing"). The next paragraph begins: "At other times it feels like being mildly drunk, or concussed. There is a sort of invisible blanket between the world and me. I find it hard to take in what anyone says." Then, a bit later: "And no one ever told me about the laziness of grief. Except at my job—where the machine seems to run on much as usual—I loathe the slightest effort.... Even shaving."[3] Such is the melting process on its emotional and attitudinal side.

Nor is that all. Our powers of discernment and discretion—of good judgment, as we say—melt down too. Richard, an experienced pastor, knew well the risks of unguarded speech, foolish action, and bad decisions while grieving, and therefore out of right-minded self-distrust he relied heavily at his time of loss on "wise friends, whose counsel I have much followed."[4] To his description of the Breviate as written "under the power of melting grief," he adds, "and therefore perhaps with the less prudent judgement; but not with the less, but the more truth; for passionate weakness poureth out all, which greater prudence may conceal.... We that are less wise tell all the truth, too little regarding how men will receive it."[5]

It is ironical that he should say this, for to pour out all he knew was his lifelong instinct, and often he had weakened rather than strengthened his persuasions, both as preacher and as politician, by not knowing when to stop; yet in this case, having implied that grief might lead him to say too much, he shows great restraint and in the end fails to tell us all we hoped to learn (about his courtship, for instance). But in his own day, when sniping at him in public and in print was so common, it was undoubtedly good advice not to share these intimate details, lest they should become matter for mockery. And it was wisdom on Richard's part to recognize that his grief might have undermined his judgment, and so to let others tell him what he should or at least what he should not put into print in the Breviate.

Despite, or because of, the melting effect of grief (readers may make up their own minds about that), Richard and Lewis each gave the world a small book forged in the furnace of grief that is frank, poignant, profound, and a lifeline for the bereaved. The two writers share the substance of the same Christian faith and are

comparably skilled with words that bring to life with clinical vivid-
ness the remarkable women they married in their own middle age,
but beyond this their books are very different. Lewis' subject is his
own experience of grieving for Joy and holding fast to his faith as
he does so, and Joy herself is predicative to that; Richard's subject
is the grace of God in Margaret, which he seeks to celebrate from
all angles, and he himself is only in the book as part of that story.
So Richard tells us more about Margaret and less about himself,
while with Lewis and Joy it is the reverse. In one respect, however,
they converge. Both were *managing* their grief (to use the standard modern word) by narrating their stories as they did, and from
this standpoint they come together as instructive examples.

The danger with grief at bereavement is that, having surren-
dered to it, as willy-nilly at first we must, we should never get
beyond it—never come out of it, never finish the grieving process.
In tribal societies, where communal solidarity is the way of living,
group mourning, ritualized to a degree and followed by a return
to the communal routines, can help those who have suffered personal loss to get back, not only functionally but emotionally too,
into the flow of ongoing reality. In the West, however, though
every family, work unit, club, and Christian congregation is tribal
to some extent, this strong solidarity in bereavement situations is a
thing of the past. The industrial revolution gave birth to the large
city, where anonymity is the rule, and to the nuclear family, whose
members, being separated from each other for most of most days,
are out of the habit of living close to each other emotionally; and
in such a milieu, for mourners to regain a life that is more than
performance while deep down the heart still aches has proved
increasingly difficult.

No wonder, then, that in recent years grief therapy, as it is called, has become a major interest in the Western world. The grief process has been studied as never before, and grief counseling has become a professional skill. The elements in grief have been thoroughly mapped: the shock, emotional collapse, panic, depression, rage, hostility, loneliness, guilt feelings, and physical symptoms that grief in bereavement may at any time involve have been monitored and criss-crossed, both in clinical counseling and in analytical literature, with a diligence that borders on the obsessional. "People have asked me if I would write about grief, because as a society we are very nervous about it," said Joanna Trollope in a press interview about her 1996 novel *Next of Kin*, and what she said was true. In our death-denying, live-forever-down-here culture we do not know how to cope with the emotional effect of a loved one's death. In such a world, grief therapy is a constant need.

The task of grief therapy is to help the bereaved past three pitfalls that yawn in their path. The first is fixation on our grief, as if we owed it to our loved ones to mourn for them for the rest of our life. Lewis saw this a generation ago as an unhealthy aberration— "All that (sometimes lifelong) ritual of sorrow—visiting graves, keeping anniversaries, leaving the empty bedroom exactly as 'the departed' used to keep it, mentioning the dead either not at all or always in a special voice, or even (like Queen Victoria) having the dead man's clothes put out for dinner every evening—this was like mummification."[6] Masquerading as respect for the dead, such behavior should rather be seen as retention of them, a psychological strategy for keeping them around us rather than letting them go. Thus it causes the sore of bereavement to go on running, so that it does not heal. This state of soul needs therapy.

The second pitfall is permanent depression, with a willed withdrawal from former involvements. Stiff-upper-lip refusal to grieve at the time of one's loss, and free fall at that time into agonized self-pity, can both produce ongoing depression, focused in the feeling that one can never live a normal life again and it would be foolish to try because one would fail. This state of mind also requires therapy.

The third pitfall is internalization of grief. This is a condition of denial in which an unfulfilled spirit of mourning, driven deep and still hurting subliminally, sours our conscious life with bitterness, cynicism, apathy, cosmic resentment, and unforgiveness of any who in any way seem to have contributed to the loved one's death. This is a further state of heart that calls for therapy.

In recent years grief counseling has become a big thing, and that is not a development to regret; but grief counseling, like marriage counseling, is not magical in its effects. Counseling can only offer understanding of what is actually going on inside and suggest what might be done about it, and just as it cannot bludgeon an estranged couple into marriage renewal, so it cannot jolly grieving persons back into cheerfulness.

People have to work their own way through their experience of grief at bereavement, and the more of themselves they had invested in the relationship and the slower-moving their temperament, the longer it will take. Real help comes from those who are there for the grieving soul in quiet friendliness, and who encourage talk about the loved one that brings forth whatever memories, regrets, guilt, and gratitude may be working in the griever's heart. Richard and Lewis, being literary men, in effect did this talking on paper, as we are seeing in full in Richard's case, but most of us need to do our talking in *viva voce* conversation. In whatever way we do it, however, expressing these things will progressively undo the bonds that tied us emotionally to the one who has gone, and so our grieving will in due course come to an end.

Two Men Grieving

For grieving was never meant to be a permanent state; it is a natural process which, if not inhibited, will run its course and from which we may hope in due time to recover. Lewis discovered this, decades before the age of grief counseling, simply by recording his thoughts and feelings as he went through it. In the final section of *A Grief Observed* he notes down his discovery, as he reviews his writing thus far:

> In so far as this record was a defense against total collapse, a safety valve, it has done some good. The other end I had in view turns out to have been based on a misunderstanding. I thought I could describe a *state*; make a map of sorrow. Sorrow, however, turns out to be not a state but a process. It needs not a map but a history.... Grief is like a long valley, a winding valley where any bend may reveal a totally new landscape. As I've already noted, not every bend does. Sometimes the surprise is the opposite one; you are presented with exactly the same sort of country you thought you had left behind miles ago. That is when you wonder whether the valley isn't a circular trench. But it isn't. There are partial recurrences, but the sequence doesn't repeat.[7]

Lewis goes on to note "two enormous gains" since he began chronicling the process: When he turns to God, he says, "my mind no longer meets that locked door" (the sense that God is silent and remote), and whereas earlier when he tried to think of Joy he was conscious only of a "vacuum," he now finds himself aware of her continuing reality. Then he writes this:

The notes have been about myself, and about [Joy], and about God. In that order. The order and the proportions exactly what they ought not to have been. And I see that I have nowhere fallen into that mode of thinking about either which we call praising them. Yet that would have been best for me. Praise is the mode of love which always has some element of joy in it. Praise in due order; of Him as the giver, of her as the gift. Don't we in praise somehow enjoy what we praise, however far we are from it? I must do more of this.... By praising I can still, in some degree, enjoy her, and already, in some degree, enjoy Him. Better than nothing.[8]

Here Lewis begins to catch up with Richard, whose memoir praises God for Margaret, and Margaret herself for her godliness, throughout.

It is worth pausing to correct the common misrepresentation of Lewis as a man who confesses that he almost lost faith in God in the early stages of his grief. This impression derives from treating his stunningly frank account of his feelings at the time as if it were a revelation of changing convictions. The error is understandable, for ours is an age in which faith in the Christian God is often treated as a matter of feeling ("What you don't feel isn't real"), rather than of facing facts that our feelings do not affect at all. But, as the most casual reader of *A Grief Observed* must see, Lewis never doubts God's reality, nor does he endorse any of the ugly fantasies about God that flit through his mind unbidden. (Ugliness and sadism, though alien to his heart, fascinated his mind from his teens on, so we need not wonder that fancyings of divine cruelty occurred to him in his grief.)

Though intellectually he was marvelously mature, in both his imaginations and his emotions he was, as his writings show, an unusual, fascinating, and fluid mixture of adult, adolescent, and child. His instincts for privacy within friendship, fantasy within realism, and concreteness within abstraction were givens; the loss of his mother to cancer when he was nine, his lifelong poor relationship with his father, and his thirty-year subservience to the masterful Mrs. Moore as to a substitute mother no doubt help to explain the form that this genetic mix took;[9] certainly, the end product was a genial, brilliant, argumentative, somewhat insecure, highly sensitive, "experiencing" person, more vulnerable to deep hurts than most.

A bachelor till his late fifties, Lewis had been married to Joy, an American Jew seventeen years younger than himself, for three years. In exploring his relationship with her he had found himself wildly happy and had rejoiced to think that there was much more to come; now, however, he had undergone the trauma of losing her—to cancer, the family bogey, which had carried off both his parents—and it is no wonder that his thoughts, feelings, and fancies ran every which way before his Christian reason, under God, could restore his Christian poise. But to tag the agony of this honest Christian lover as loss of faith is crass, and wrong.

Back, now, to Richard. He wrote the Breviate, as we have seen, "under the power of melting grief," "in some passion indeed of love and grief, but in sincerity of truth."[10] From the fact that his friend John Howe, preaching Margaret's funeral sermon, said: "You will have her just memorial more at large e'er long,"[11] it would seem that Richard planned "this paper monument"[12] as soon as Margaret died. That should not surprise us, for he had dabbled in edifying biography before and valued it greatly as a spiritually fruitful form of writing; and Margaret herself had become well known and admired for her efforts, as a nonconforming minor aristocrat with some cash, to support Richard's ministry and so advance the gospel. What we should notice here, however, is that composing the Breviate was perhaps the most therapeutic thing Richard could have done for the managing of the grief process in his own life.

It is fascinating to compare Richard and Lewis at this point. It looks as if Richard was a more integrated man emotionally than Lewis was. And as a pastor in an era when people died at home, when half the children born died young, and when average life expectancy was less than forty years, Richard was undoubtedly more used to dealing with death than was the Oxbridge don. But beyond all that, there is a calm matter-of-factness and an almost clinical sobriety in Richard's telling of Margaret's story that contrasts strikingly with the terse, choppy style of Lewis' cries from the emotional deeps in which he found himself. Granted, *A Grief Observed*, which he published under a pseudonym to help people, consists of disconnected jottings, written at irregular intervals (though carefully arranged, I think, for the press); however, a sense of strain, more or less, marks them all, and there is no strain in Richard's book. At a guess, therefore (it cannot be more), lover Richard was able to handle his grief more smoothly than lover Lewis, and this (I guess again) was for four reasons.

First, Richard's long-ingrained mental habit of viewing all life, death included, *sub specie aeternitatis* (from the standpoint of eternity: that is, in two-worldly terms, with this world seen as a path of pilgrimage to that world) stood him in good stead when Margaret was taken from him. Though Lewis' apologetic and fictional writings contain wonderfully evocative pictures of heaven in a way that makes him unique among this century's Christian writers, in *A Grief Observed* we find him distrusting all his imaginations, viewing God as the great iconoclast who must and does destroy them, and declaring ignorance about the life beyond. However discerning such agnosticism might be, it left him to wonder about Joy's unknown condition and possible accessibility to him after her death in a way that has no parallel in the Breviate. Richard trusts the biblical pictures of heaven as the perfect society of the perfected godly, enjoying their Lord and each other in endless joy and delight, and quietly looks forward to rejoining Margaret there.

Second, by presenting Margaret to his readers as an object lesson in faith and faithfulness, Richard resumed his public identity as preacher, teacher, and pastor. This would have renewed his sense of the meaningfulness of his ongoing life and so acted as a counterweight to the enervating down-drag of his inward distress. Though *A Grief Observed* was also published to help people (specifically, bereaved believers), it is essentially its author's personal story of moving through mourning, not an object lesson in any sense, and so it would have had less therapeutic significance in Lewis' grief experience.

Third, Richard believed that as he had never deserved God's gift of Margaret during their years of life together, so God's withdrawal of the gift was no more than he deserved for his failures in discipleship and devotion. "The Lord gave, and the Lord hath taken away; and he hath taken away but that upon my desert, which he had given me undeservedly near nineteen years."[13] "In 1681, God called my sin to remembrance by his heavy hand on my dear wife, a woman of extraordinary acuteness of wit, solidity of judgment, incredible prudence and sagacity, and sincere devotedness to God ... who had heaped on me so many and great obligations to love and tenderness as made my wound more deep and painful. She had a hot, sharp blood and hot brain, and a woman persuading her to too long a use of ginger for the colic had cast her into a distraction [mental disorientation] three years before; and I had begged and obtained her speedy recovery of God and promised a better usage and improvement of so great a mercy, but broke my vows and made no better use of it than before."[14]

This humbling sense that Margaret was always more, and losing her was never more, than he deserved cut off at the root the anger at God for letting the loved one die which is so frequently an element in the grieving of religious people today. Lewis shares rich thoughts about the parting of couples through death as part of God's plan for their perfecting (he thinks the matter out in terms of belief in a sanctifying purgatory, but those who, like me, do not share this belief can easily make the adjustment): the thoughts would, however, be richer still were Richard's sense of deserving none of the good gifts of earthly marriage their frame, and possibly Lewis' inner turmoil as he sought to adjust to losing Joy would in that case have been less.

Fourth, Richard expected his own death very soon. "She is gone after many of my choicest friends, who within this one year are gone to Christ, and I am following even at the door.... I am going after them to that blessed society where life, light, and love, and therefore harmony, concord, and joy, are perfect and everlasting."[15] "I am waiting to be next."[16] Richard, who had thought of himself from the age of twenty as living with one foot in the grave,[17] was at this time in such a feeble state that his expectation of death was quite natural, and his long-standing habit of daily meditation on heaven, to make the prospect of future glory vivid to his mind and exciting to his heart,[18] must have given the expectation a comforting and healing effect upon him as he grieved for his temporarily lost spouse. "She cried out to me, 'My mother is in heaven,… and thou and I shall be in heaven.'"[19]

Richard was not to know that his life would continue for another decade; he anticipated fulfillment of Margaret's deathbed words much sooner, and ministered to his own grief by thinking and writing accordingly. Lewis, however, lost Joy almost a year before he was diagnosed with the heart and kidney problems that were soon to end his life, so nothing like Richard's expectation appears in *A Grief Observed*. Lewis, rather, is facing the prospect of many years as a widower—a tougher assignment altogether, emotionally speaking.

Richard Remembers Margaret

Now we shall follow Richard, as best we can, through his actual writing of the Breviate.

His defensively titled final chapter, "Some Uses Proposed to the Reader from This History, as the Reasons Why I Wrote It," gives us the clue to his standpoint in memorializing the woman he had loved. The lessons he drew from Margaret's story, writes Keeble, "amount to the contention that his wife's experiences can encourage hope, discourage despair, and prevent false expectations by showing what a saint may expect in this world, and that her examples may guide others."[20]

More precisely, Richard uses her story to illustrate, first, the credibility of the biblical gospel, which proclaims the supernaturalism of the Christian life as Margaret, like others, had lived it; second, the struggles, trials, and imperfections of the godly; third, the roots of sorrow and of joy in the spiritual life; fourth, the burdens that come with the blessings of marriage, especially to ministers; fifth, the security of believers as they die and pass into glory. These were evidently the angles of vision on which, as Margaret's loving husband, faithful pastor, and best friend for nineteen years, Richard fixed his mind as he looked over documents in Margaret's hand (some of which he had not seen before) and ordered his own memories in preparation for the writing itself; for it is from these angles that he actually narrates Margaret's life.

The first lesson he resolves to draw from Margaret's story is a large one. He thinks his account of her as a person of "sincere devotedness to God, and unusual strict obedience to him,"[21] should show skeptics that they are wrong to imagine the Bible to be untrue, and "holiness, as it differs from heathen morality, to be but fancy, hypocrisy, custom, or self-conceit": in other words, an unreality and a fraud. "A man that never felt the working of God's special grace in his own heart is hardly brought to believe that others have that which he never had himself.... But acquaintance, if intimate with gracious persons, might convince them of their moral error; and true history methinks may do much toward it."[22]

The anti-Puritan backlash and the Pelagian type of moralism that had anchored themselves in the Church of England since the Restoration had generated deep doubts about the reality of the new birth and the lasting change of motive and character to which it gives rise: but lives like Margaret's must surely explode the skepticism and confirm the truth of the biblical message. Richard broadens this point in a personal way. Being skeptical himself by nature, he had in the past struggled over the truth of the Bible, and now cherished "several firsthand experiences or present certainties which have been a great succor to my faith, to save me from temptations to unbelief and doubting and confirm my assurance that the Scripture is God's Word." He feels and sees Scripture verified, he tells us, not only in its account of "the renewing work of the Holy Ghost and the spiritual difference of the sanctified from others," but also in its descriptive diagnosis of original sin as the universal human condition, and of the endless enmity between "the serpent's and the holy seed" (the world and the people of God), and of "all the temptations of Satan, and the secret war within us between the spirit and the flesh." Furthermore, he sees Scripture fulfilled in its promise of "a blessing on God's Word and his ordinances"; "even as it persuadeth me the easilier to believe that there are devils, when I see their very nature and works in devils incarnate,... and to believe that there is a hell when I see so much of hell on earth."[23]

In planning to say all this, has he lost sight of his focal theme, Margaret's holy life? Not really; for it is clear that he is thinking back to the way Margaret's life was changed under his ministry in Kidderminster, and then to the bitterness, backbiting, and brutality that nonconformists like themselves had to endure during the previous two decades, and that formed the milieu within which Margaret's Christian sweetness, cheerfulness, and patience had to be, and wonderfully were, maintained. Here, as Richard saw it, was a triumph of grace, and he planned to tell the story in a way that would bring this out. The same realism and honesty that would keep him from hiding the morbid and unbalanced streaks in her character would lead him to highlight these victories of supernatural Christlikeness in her conduct. Nowhere does Richard actually call her a holy woman, but that is the phrase that springs to mind as we read his narrative tribute to her memory: a tribute in which, surely according to his plan, the transforming impact of God's grace upon her is made to stand out in extremely bold relief.

The second lesson that Richard aimed to enforce from Margaret's story was also a large one, namely that struggles, temptations, and constant imperfect performance mark the lives of all God's saints. In their quest for obedience to God, which is and must ever be their main concern, they have to cope with distractions, deceptions, perversities, and pitfalls all the way, all the time. Both the peace of not having problems and the perfection of being totally free from sin are blessings that belong to the next world; here, our sanctification is incomplete, our obedience is always flawed, and our spiritual reach regularly exceeds our spiritual grasp. The thought is many-sided, but its key facets are these:

Take heed of expecting too much from so frail and bad a thing as man.... They that come near us find more faults and badness in us than others at a distance know.... It is too common an error with honest souls to think that a hard heart lieth most in want of sorrow and tears, when as it lieth most in want of a tractable compliance and yielding to the commands and will of God,... and to think that a new and tender heart is principally a heart that can weep and mourn, when it is chiefly a heart that easily receiveth all the impressions of God's commands and promises and threats, and easily yieldeth to his known will.

...Fear and avoid self-willedness.... We must learn to follow and not to lead, and to say: *The will of the Lord be done; not mine, Lord, but thine;* and in every estate to be content. There is no rest but in God's will. [A lesson Margaret had to learn at Kidderminster, before they were married.]

...God's service lieth more in deeds than in words. My dear wife was faulty indeed in talking so little of religion in company.... But her religion lay in doing more than talk. Yet her example tells us that it is one of Satan's wiles to draw us to one sin to avoid another ... and leave much undone for fear of doing it amiss....

...It is not God's or our enemies' afflicting us in worldly losses or sufferings (especially when we suffer for righteousness' sake) which is half so painful as our own inward infirmities.... My poor wife made nothing of prisons, distrainings, reproaches, and such crosses, but her burden was most inward, from her own tenderness, and next from those whom she over-loved. And for mine own part, all that ever either enemies or friends have done against me is but a flea-biting to me in comparison of the daily burden of a pained body and the weakness of my soul in faith, hope, love, and heavenly desires and delights.[24]

The nature of true religion, holiness, obedience, and all duty to God and man was printed in her conceptions, in so clear and distinct a character as made her ... look at greater exactness than I and such as I could reach.... And in this respect she was the meetest helper that I could have had;... for I was apt to be over-careless in my speech and too backward to my duty, and she was always endeavoring to bring me to greater wariness and strictness in both. If I spoke rashly or sharply, it offended her; if I behaved (as I was apt) with too much neglect of ceremony or humble compliment to any, she would modestly tell me of it; if my very looks seemed not pleasant, she would have me amend them

(which my weak pained state of body undisposed me to do);
if I forgot any week to catechize my servants and familiarly
instruct them personally (besides my ordinary family
duties),[25] she was troubled at my remissness.[26]

Richard's purpose of writing "true history" led him to recount
Margaret's weaknesses, flaws, and struggles alongside her
strengths, virtues, and achievements. He does not present her as a
plaster saint but as a born-again servant of God with a heart of
gold, feet of clay, and huge natural vulnerabilities. His two
chapters, "Of Her Exceeding Desires to Do Good" and "Of Her
Qualifications and Infirmities," give us an utterly fascinating pen-
portrait, humble, factual, discerning, and affectionate throughout,
of the complex, brilliant, highly strung, delicate, secretive, passionate, restless, loyal, managing woman that Margaret was.

"A good wife contains so many persons in herself," wrote
Lewis. Joy "was my daughter and my mother, my pupil and my
teacher, my subject and my sovereign; and always, holding all this
in solution, my trusty comrade, friend, shipmate, fellow-soldier.
My mistress; but at the same time all that any man friend (and I
have good ones) has ever been to me. Perhaps more."[27] Plainly, as
Joy was all this to Lewis, so was Margaret to Richard, and Richard,
like Lewis, had a flair for focusing the three-dimensional humanity
of his much younger mate.

So mercurial Margaret, with her vigorous initiatives, sweet
restraint with her servants, twice-monthly migraines and recurring
chest congestion, and permanent hidden fears of all sorts fueled by
nightmare memories[28] and frequent actual nightmares (worry
dreams "of fire and murderers"[29]), springs to uncannily vivid life
under the grieving widower's pen. Pastor Richard having decided

to save the theological evaluations till the end of the book, husband Richard is free in these chapters to use his memories and insights to present her as she was—"warts and all," as Oliver Cromwell once put it. The result is a little masterpiece of character drawing.

Here, for instance, we learn that Margaret's Christian passion to do good to others lacked a sense of proportion, so that she would stretch her generosity beyond the bounds of prudence, "over-love" relatives, friends, and those she admired, overexert herself almost obsessively on cherished projects (e.g., keeping Richard preaching), and then be prostrated with disappointment when people and events did not come up to her expectations. "If these whom she over-loved had not been as good and done as well as she would have them, in innocent behavior, in piety, and (if rich) in liberality, it over-troubled her, and she could not bear it. She was apt when she set her mind and heart upon some good work ... to be too much pleased in her ... self-made promises of the success, and then almost overturned with trouble when they disappointed her.... Her will was set upon good, but her weakness could not bear the crossing and frustration of it."[30]

Here also we learn of her built-in perfectionism (that is what a modern psychologist would surely call it). It led her to insist on keeping a spotless house; it totally inhibited her from speaking in a group about Christian truth and experience and from taking family prayers when Richard was away, for fear her performance would be hypocritical; it moved her to wish that Richard would write fewer books, and write those fewer better; and it made her very hard on Richard when she felt he had not behaved perfectly in company or toward her personally.

Here, too, we learn of her "diseased fearfulness against which she had little more free will or power than a man in an ague or frost against shaking cold."[31] Because of this "uncurable timorousness,"[32] a slamming door, "or anything that had suddenness, noise, or fierceness in it,"[33] or violent arguments, or bad news, upset her: basically, because she feared these things would unhinge her mind. Richard admits: "I was apt to think it was but a passionate fanciful fear, and was too apt to be impatient with her impatiency and with every trouble of her mind, not enough considering how great tenderness ... she needed."[34]

On the big matters of faith and obedience, she lived fearlessly: "I took it for an evidence of the power of grace," writes Richard, "that so timorous a person had overcome most of her fears of hell and God's desertion and was more fearless of persecution, imprisonment, or losses and poverty thereby, than I or any that I remember to have known."[35] Yet for over twenty years Margaret lived with the haunting fear that her mind would give way, and for her last three years she was sure she had breast cancer, so that she dieted and starved herself to keep it at bay while she "prepared constantly for a sad death";[36] as in fact she was doing at the time of her last illness. "Diseased fearfulness" indeed! The fearless faith of one so irrationally fearful by nature was, as Richard wrote, a true triumph of grace, for which there was every reason to praise God.

The portrait being drawn for us is of a young to middle-aged upper-class woman with a strong mind, strong feelings, quick reactions, vast nervous energy, and great inner complexity. Childless herself, she is enterprising, outgoing, and untiring in seeking to arrange things well for her husband, her relatives, and others for whom she cares. By nature she is a bundle of obsessive fears and neurotic fancies, yet her faith keeps her heart fundamentally carefree, even when she is most deeply in the toils of her temperament, and she is able to conceal her anxieties (too well, perhaps) and be consistently charming and winning in her ways. She is devoted to the chronically ill, irritable, overworking clergyman whom she has married and takes in stride the disruptions and bad experiences that now perforce she shares with him. In the invidious circumstances of her everyday life she struggles most bravely to honor God and live to his praise, in terms of the convictions that are common to her husband and herself.

The widower-writer of the Breviate celebrates her courage without suggesting that her firmness of purpose guaranteed wisdom and steadiness and flawless performance; he saw, and lets us see, that it did not. But recollecting and recording that firmness of purpose, and inviting his readers to admire the strength of her loyalty to her spouse and to her God, is clearly a solace to Richard's sorrowing soul, as appears from the loving detail with which he actually does it.

Third, Richard is anxious to draw a lesson for everyone from his account of Margaret's spiritual journey out of depression and despair into a peace and confidence that quelled her obsessive fears, at least for much of the time. He makes his point by underlining his typical Puritan certainty (yes, *typical* is correct!) that joy is the ordinary condition of healthy believers, and by celebrating the fact that Margaret's overall temper was one of Christian joy, despite the occasional depressive intrusions. "The fears and penitent sorrows, which foolishly fleshly sinners fly from, do tend to everlasting peace and joy [he refers to the strains and pains of true conversion, which the first part of the Breviate illustrates]; and perfect love will cast out all tormenting fears, unless it be those of a timorous diseased temper which have more of sickness than of sin and will be laid aside with the body, which was their cause."[37]

It is Richard's strong conviction that "holiness lies especially in delighting in God, his Word and works, and in his joyful praise and hopes of glory.... Religion consists in doing God's commanding will ... and joyfully trusting in his promising and disposing will.... Fear and sorrow are but to ... further all this."[38] This teaching had sustained him personally over many years of frustration and disappointment as he adjusted to the fact that the comprehensive, evangelical Church of England for which he had worked and prayed was never to be; he had seen the same teaching change Margaret's life, and now he wants it to influence all readers of the Breviate, too. Though, as he tells us, he writes the Breviate in grief and sorrow, it is hardly too much to describe restful joy in God as its subtext throughout.

The fourth reality on which Richard's mind homed as he thought about the "uses" of Margaret's story was marriage itself. As we saw earlier, in Puritan marriage roles and responsibilities were laid out very fully, and moderns, seeing this, easily assume that the personal depth and closeness of the relationship must have suffered as a result. Popular culture today treats structure in relationships as restrictive rather than liberating, and impoverishing rather than enriching. Popular culture, however, is at this point wrong. Though set patterning determines the style of a relationship, it need not in any way restrict the rapport that builds within the pattern, and that rapport can be more substantial than ever it would be without the pattern.

It was so in Richard's and Margaret's case. As they well studied and diligently did their marital "duties," their bonding became very solid, and their affection and respect for each other became huge. "You see here," writes Richard, "that suitableness in religious judgment and disposition preserveth faster love and concord (as it did with us) than suitableness in age, education, and wealth.... Nothing causeth so near and fast and comfortable a union as to be united in one God, one Christ, one Spirit, one church, one hope of heavenly glory."[39] That was profoundly true when Richard wrote it, and it is just as true—just as precious a lesson, therefore—today.

Richard learned to entrust to Margaret all domestic, financial, and business arrangements. "Her apprehension of such things was so much quicker and more discerning than mine, that though I was naturally somewhat tenacious of my own conceptions, her reasons and my experience usually told me that she was in the right and knew more than I. She would at the first hearing understand the matter better than I could do by many and long thoughts.... In very hard cases about what was to be done, she would suddenly open all the way what was to be opened, in the things of the family, estate, or any civil business.... Experience acquainted her that I knew less in such things than she, and therefore was willing she should take it all upon her."[40] She showed herself, as we would say, a very competent business woman, and Richard appreciated her as such.

Margaret's contribution to Richard's ministry went further than trying to arrange for him to preach and teach and refraining from interrupting him while he studied and wrote. When they married, she consented to "expect none of my time which my ministerial work should require,"[41] and the priority of his ministerial concerns became a rule of the house. "My conscience hath forced me many times to omit secret prayer with my wife when she desired it, for want of time, not daring to omit far greater work."[42] "Of late years ... my writings, preachings, and other public duty (which I ever thought I was bound to prefer before lesser) did so wholly take up those few hours of the day which I had out of my bed" (because of "constant weakness and pain") "that I was seldomer in secret prayer with my wife than she desired."[43] Margaret thought he would have done better to write less and pray with her and minister directly in their home rather more, but "I thought there were many to do such work that would not do mine, and that I chose the greatest, which I durst not omit, and could not do both in the measure that I desired else to have done."[44] Margaret, however reluctantly, accepted this.

In one branch of his ministry, though, Richard recruited Margaret's direct help. "Cases of conscience"—questions, that is, about the fittest and best course of action for one who wants to please God—came Richard's way in abundance, and once he had discovered that Margaret was brilliant at dealing with such questions he regularly sought her advice about them. "She was better at resolving a case of conscience than most divines that ever I knew in all my life. I often put cases to her which she suddenly so resolved as to convince me of some degree of oversight in my own resolution. Insomuch that of late years, I confess, that I was used to put all, save secret [i.e., confidential] cases, to her and hear what she could say. Abundance of difficulties were brought me, some about restitution, some about injuries, some about references, some about vows, some about marriage promises, and many such like; and she would lay all the circumstances presently together, compare them, and give me a more exact resolution than I could do."[45] It is clear that in their partnership Richard and Margaret each relied on and enjoyed what the other could do. The relationship was fulfilling and fulfilled in every sense.

After all this, it comes as a shock when Richard lapses, in his chapter on the uses of Margaret's story, into what for him was a familiar routine—decrying pastors' marriages. He had been criticized as inconsistent for himself marrying after going on record with the view that clerical marriage, while not sinful, should be eschewed wherever possible: the insinuation apparently was that he had forsaken his principles in order to marry Margaret for her money. Stung, Richard responds that he still holds his earlier view, that the pastorate requires a freedom from care that family responsibilities regularly rule out, "and I have never changed my judgment. Yea, my wife lived and died in the same mind."[46] (Did Richard kid himself here? One wonders; but certainly he wrote in good faith.) As he has already explained, he would never have considered marriage had he not been barred from the pastorate by the Restoration settlement, and when he married he explicitly renounced all interest in Margaret's patrimony, "that I ... might not seem to marry her for covetousness."[47]

So he was entitled to be indignant at the malicious gossip; but in his indignation, as so often, he does not know when to stop and launches into a diatribe against pastors' marriages which depends for its strength on the assumption that they will be poor men who choose poor quality wives—hardly the happiest note to strike at that point. But Richard, like Margaret, had the weakness of his strengths, and for better or for worse debating was one of his strengths. What he wanted to get across, I think, judging by his teaching on marriage which we reviewed earlier, was that marriage, even at its best, brings its blessings within a frame of burdensome cares, which easily put a married pastor at a disadvantage. From the way he writes, however, you would think his purpose was to censure as thoughtless fools clergy who marry when they have no continence problem and to evoke pity for those who marry for chastity's sake, as being willy-nilly hamstrung in their ministry. We should simply note that this is the only bit of the Breviate that can in any sense be called a lapse, and having said that, move on.

The last lesson that Richard would have us learn from Margaret's story, one that was very familiar ground for Puritan teachers, is the theology of the deathbed. The Puritan hope (it could be no more) was that one's deathbed would be a time when the reality of the next world, and the nearness of the Christ who had now come to take his servant into it, would become specially vivid. Words of special wisdom and confidence might then be spoken from a personal Mount Nebo, as the dying soul gazed on dawning glory like Moses gazing at the promised land. Such a hope is, of course, generically Christian rather than specifically Puritan, and Lewis (for instance) is glad to be able to record that his wife's last words ("not to me but to the chaplain") were "I am at peace with God."[48]

But it did not always happen that way, and Margaret had died in a state of partial delirium. "Though her understanding never perfectly returned, she ... oft showed us that her soul did work toward God.... She desired me to pray by her, and seemed quietly to join to the end. She heard divers psalms, and a chapter read, and repeated part, and sung part of a psalm herself. The last words that she spoke were: 'My God, help me! Lord, have mercy upon me!' God had been so many years training her up under the expectation and preparations for death, as made the case of her soul less grievous to me, as no way doubting of her salvation."[49]

The lesson to be learned is as follows:

As God's servants have not their portion or good things in this life, so they may have the same sicknesses and manner of death as others.... There is no judging of a man's sincerity or of his future state by his disease or by his diseased death-bed words. He that liveth to God shall die safely into the hand of God, though a fever or delirium hinder him from knowing this, till experience and sudden possession of heaven convince him.[50]

A Marriage Fulfilled

Every marriage is different, for every couple is different, and whatever ideas they start with they have to find their own way into the mutually enriching relationship that they rightly seek. Richard and Margaret, the workaholic pastor and the willful rich girl, started with the Puritan idea of marriage and built their relationship on that basis with spectacular success. As we can now see, they loved each other realistically, neither idolizing nor idealizing each other.

Lewis, exploring the fancy that the dead know the living more clearly, wrote: "Does [Joy] now see exactly how much froth or tinsel there was in what she called, and I call, my love? So be it. Look your hardest, dear. I wouldn't hide if I could. We didn't idealize each other. We tried to keep no secrets. You knew most of the rotten places in me already. If you now see anything worse, I can take it. So can you. Rebuke, explain, mock, forgive. For this is one of the miracles of love; it gives … a power of seeing through its own enchantments and yet not being disenchanted."[51]

Clearly the realistic, resilient love of which Lewis writes is a love that Richard and Margaret also knew. Vividly aware of each other's faults, they loved each other just the same, ever thankful for having each other and ever eager to give to each other. In this they were a model of maturity in marriage.

Richard prints what we would call a love letter from himself to

Margaret, written after they had been married for three years. It anchors their love in God throughout and works up to saying: "The Lord forgive my great unprofitableness and the sin that brought me under any disabilities to answer your earnest and honest desires of greater helps than I afford you, and help me yet to amend it toward you."[52] Introducing it, Richard states: "I reproduce this ... partly ... as an act of repentance for those failings of her just expectations.... For though she oft said that before she married me she expected more sourness and unsuitableness than she found; yet I am sure that she found less zeal and holiness and strictness in all words and looks and duties, and less help for her soul, than she expected." He continues wryly, she learned that "grace doth stand with more faultiness than she had imagined,"[53] and so was helped to lay hold of her own Christian identity as a sinner living by being forgiven, just like her husband. So the marriage prospered, with both Richard and Margaret humbly acknowledging their shortcomings and trying to do something about them, until the lovers were parted by Margaret's death.

The Sanctifying of Grief

Now that we have tracked the main lessons Richard thought should be learned from Margaret's life story, we return to the theme of managing (modern word) and sanctifying (Puritan word) the grief experience—an activity to which I have already suggested that Richard's writing of the Breviate belongs. I now give a summary account of this activity, in Puritan terms (which, let me say at once, I endorse).

All life, said the Puritans, must be managed in such a way that it is sanctified; that is, all activities must be performed, and all experi-

ences received and responded to, in a way that honors God, benefits others as far as possible, and helps us forward in our knowledge
and enjoyment of God here as we travel home to the glory of
heaven hereafter. Of the experiences to be sanctified, some are
pleasant and some are painful. The Puritan labels for the latter are
"afflictions" and "crosses"; and bereavement, with the grief it
brings, is one such.

How may an experience be sanctified? By relating it to the truth
of the gospel, so that we understand it in biblical and evangelical
terms; by letting it remind us of truths we might otherwise forget,
or not take seriously; and by disciplining our hearts to accept it in
an appropriate way—with gratitude or self-humbling or whatever.

Of what truths particularly should the bereavement experience
remind us? Said the Puritans characteristically, the three that follow:

1. The reality of God's sovereignty—that we, like everyone else,
are always in his hands, and neither bereavement nor anything else
occurs apart from his overruling will.

2. The reality of our own mortality—that we, like everyone else,
are not in this world on a permanent basis and must sooner or later
leave it for another mode of existence under other conditions.

3. The reality of heaven and hell—that we leave this world for
one or the other, and that we should use the time God gives us
here to ensure that as saved sinners we shall go to heaven, rather
than as unsaved sinners go to hell.

To what exercises of mind and heart (attitudes and actions)
should the bereavement experience lead us? Said the Puritans characteristically, these three:

1. The exercise of thanksgiving for all that we valued and
enjoyed in the person we have lost and, in the case of a believer, for

the happiness to which we know that he or she has now been promoted.

2. The exercise of submission to God, as we resign to him the loved one he has taken from us, confess to him that we had no claim on the continuance of that loved one's earthly life, and consciously put ourselves in his hands for whatever future experiences he has in mind for us.

3. The exercise of patience, which is a compound of endurance and hope, as we live through our bereavement on a daily basis.

Richard, in his sadness at losing Margaret, transparently models all three in the Breviate. Lewis, mourning the loss of Joy, does the same in *A Grief Observed.*

Grief, the experiential, emotional fruit of the bereavement event, is, as we have seen, a state of desolation and isolation, of alternating apathy and agony, of inner emptiness and exhaustion. How may such a condition be sanctified—that is, managed, lived with, and lived through, in a way that honors God? No Puritan to my knowledge addresses the question in this form, but the Puritan answer would be this:

Starting from where you are, do what you can (it may not be much at first) to move toward the thanksgiving, submission, and patience of which we have just heard.

Do not let your grief loosen your grip on the goodness and grace of your loving Lord.

Cry (for there is nothing biblical or Christian, or indeed human, about the stiff upper lip).

Tell God your sadness (several of the psalms, though not written about bereavement, will supply words for the purpose).

Pray as you can, and don't try to pray as you can't. (That bit of wisdom is not original to me, nor was it distilled in a grief counseling context, but it is very apropos here.)

Avoid well-wishers who think they can cheer you up, but thank God for any who are content to be with you and do things for you without talking at you.

Talk to yourself (or, like Richard, write) about the loved one you lost.

Do not try to hurry your way out of the inner weakness you feel; grieving takes time.

Look to God as thankfully, submissively, and patiently as you can (and he will understand if you have to tell him that you cannot really do this yet).

Feel, acknowledge, and face, consciously and from your heart, all the feelings that you find in yourself at present, and the day will come when you find yourself able, consciously and from your heart, to live to God daily in thanksgiving, submission, and patient hope once again; as did Richard, and Lewis, and millions more.

Grieving properly leads back to thinking properly, living properly, and praising properly. God sees to that! "Blessed are those who mourn, for they will be comforted" (Matt. 5:4).

Epilogue

To the Reader,
Once More

WHY DID I PUT THIS BOOK TOGETHER? For three reasons.

First, I wanted you to meet Richard Baxter. Through his writings he has been a close personal friend of mine for over half a century, and I wanted to share him. An outstanding pastoral evangelist, a gifted and prolific devotional writer, and a major prophet (unheeded, unfortunately) to the Anglican Church in the second half of the seventeenth century, he is endlessly interesting; for beyond his public roles he was a great and communicative human being who lets you hear his heart beat as he writes. Other authors have felt his fascination and presented him in print from various standpoints; I wanted to introduce him to you as a husband working at his Puritan marriage, and as a widower grieving for the lively lady who had been his life-partner for almost twenty years. I also wanted you to meet her, in the extraordinarily vivid and perceptive account of her that Richard gives. They were two memorable Christian people with whom I would have loved to spend time (maybe in heaven that will be possible; I hope so), and I thought that when you had met them through Richard's memoir you would feel about them as I do. They enrich my life; I should like them to enrich yours, too.

Second, I wanted you to know about the Puritan ideal for marriage and to see how it differs from what is usual in the West today. For Richard and Margaret, as for the whole Bible-based Puritan movement, marriage was a covenant partnership meant to be God-centered and lifelong, a privilege, a calling, and a task. One married "for better for worse, for richer for poorer," as the sixteenth-century Book of Common Prayer classically put it: circumstantial problems and pressures were certain, so one must choose one's partner carefully, in the knowledge that supporting each other through troubles would be a major part of the matrimonial task, and one needed a partner with resources for doing that, just as one must expect and prepare to be regularly doing it oneself. Very different is the secular modern attitude—"the purpose of my marriage is to meet my needs, and the basis for it is the prospect of a satisfying sex life, and should the purpose or basis fail I will end my marriage by divorce, so that I can try again with someone else." I wanted you to be able to compare and contrast the two ideals and to ask yourself not only which is the more biblical and Christian (not a hard question to answer, I think) but which in practice is more truly human and more truly humane.

Third, I wanted you to see something of the Christian way of handling the grief that bereavement brings. The secular grief counseling of today is of little help here. Secular theory commonly expects the bereaved to feel rage at their loss and to be angry with God, if they believe in God, for letting it happen. Secular theory seems to suppose that Christians expect their faith to shield them from suffering, pain, all forms of loss, and in particular the death of anyone they care for, so that they will feel bereavement as a threat to their belief and an occasion for panic anger, in which the question *why* will become a stone thrown at God repeatedly. No doubt some self-styled Christians feel and act like this, but such reactions are not biblical or Christian any more than is the idea that the life of faith will be trouble-free. Richard models the Christian path through grief when he reaffirms, to himself as well as to his readers, the good, wise, and just sovereignty of God. This is the meaning of his echo of Job 1:21: "The Lord gave, and the Lord hath taken away; and he hath taken away but that upon my desert, which he had given me undeservedly near nineteen years. Blessed be the name of the Lord."

As the first half of Richard's tribute to Margaret is a beacon for all who would find God, and the second half is an inspiration for all who are married, so Richard's own attitude permeating the whole book, and made explicit by such passages as that just quoted, is a lifeline for all bereaved grievers. I wanted to put this lifeline in your hands, for the day will come when you, as well as I, will need it.

Richard buried Margaret in her mother's tomb. Ever the evangelist, he had written the following verse to be inscribed on it:

Thus must thy flesh to silent dust descend,
Thy mirth and worldly pleasure thus will end:
Then happy, holy souls, but woe to those
Who heaven forgot, and earthly pleasures chose:
Hear now this preaching grave without delay,
Believe, repent, and work while it is day.

I want to leave you with this. Doggerel? Yes, certainly. Gospel? Yes, just as certainly. A word in season? A message, whether well expressed or not, for our time? Think about it, and give your own answer to my question.

Notes

Prologue

1. Below, 136.
2. F.J. Powicke, *The Reverend Richard Baxter under the Cross (1662-1691)* (London: Jonathan Cape, 1927), 275; citing a passage in Baxter's autobiography (*Reliquiae Baxterianae,* ed. Matthew Sylvester, 1696; hereafter RB) that the original editor suppressed.
3. Below, 56.
4. Baxter's narrative, published as *A Breviate of the Life of Margaret, The Daughter of Francis Charlton,...Esq; And Wife of Richard Baxter* (1681), was reprinted with introduction, notes, and appendices by John T. Wilkinson as *Richard Baxter and Margaret Charlton: A Puritan Love-Story* (London: George Allen & Unwin, 1928). Appreciations of it can be found in Powicke, 100-108 and *passim*; J.M. Lloyd-Thomas, ed., *The Autobiography of Richard Baxter* (London: J.M. Dent & Sons, 1925), 267-77; N.H. Keeble, *Richard Baxter: Puritan Man of Letters* (Oxford: Clarendon Press, 1982), 127-31.
5. *Practical Works of Richard Baxter* (Ligonier, Pa.: Soli Deo Gloria, 1990-91), IV:1002-12 ("A Sermon Preached at the Funeral of that Faithful Minister of Christ, Mr. John Corbet. With his True and Exemplary Character").
6. Keeble, 128.
7. Keeble, 127. Lloyd-Thomas, 268, calls it "incomparable"; Powicke, 101, refers to it as "this gem of biography."
8. He knew that it was a phrase Baxter had used: see C.S. Lewis, *Mere Christianity* (London: Collins, Fontana Books, 1955), 6.
9. Lewis, 12.
10. George Sayer, *Jack,* 2d ed. (Wheaton, Ill.: Crossway, 1994), 393.
11. E.g., Sheldon Vanauken, *A Severe Mercy* (New York: Harper & Row, 1977); Nicholas Wolterstorff, *Lament for a Son* (Grand Rapids, Mich.: Eerdmans, 1987); Luci Shaw, *God in the Dark* (Grand Rapids, Mich.: Zondervan/ Broadmoor, 1989); Rick Taylor, *When Life Is Changed Forever* (Eugene, Ore.: Harvest House, 1992); Mary A. White, *Harsh Grief, Gentle Hope* (Colorado Springs: NavPress, 1995).

Part I
Great Gladness

1. 97-98.

2. 65.

3. 60.

4. April 10, 1660; 75.

5. It was a foregone conclusion that the restoration of the English monarchy in 1660 would entail the re-establishing of the Church of England with its episcopacy and Prayer Book in something like its post-Reformation Elizabethan form, which the Long Parliament had proscribed in 1645. Monarchist, protagonist for a territorial national church, and Puritan spokesman and publicist, Baxter went to London to campaign for a religious settlement comprehensive enough to include clergy like himself, a campaign which he continued for the rest of his life.

6. 57.

7. The 1660 Act for Confirming and Restoring of Ministers had replaced Baxter by the nonpreaching vicar George Dance, who was there before Baxter arrived in 1641. Bishop Morley of Worcester then refused Baxter a license to preach anywhere in his diocese. Already in 1660 Baxter could see that the comprehensive national church, including Puritan clergy, that he sought was very unlikely to materialize. The 1662 Act of Uniformity, which led to the ejection from parish ministry of nearly two thousand Puritan clergy, culminated a two-year process of sectarian Anglican revenge.

8. 100.

9. I have described historical Puritanism more fully in *A Quest for Godliness* (Wheaton, Ill.: Crossway, 1990; published in Britain as *Among God's Giants*, Eastbourne: Kingsway, 1990). See also Leland Ryken, *Worldly Saints: The Puritans as they Really Were* (Grand Rapids, Mich.: Zondervan, 1986).

10. Wilkinson, 43.

11. See *A Quest for Godliness*, chapter sixteen, "Marriage and Family in Puritan Thought," 259-73.

12. Wilkinson, 43-44.

13. The phrase quoted is from a sentence in George Whitefield's letter to Mr. and Mrs. Delamotte asking for their daughter's hand in marriage: the full sentence reads, "I bless God, if I know anything of my own heart, I am free from that foolish passion which the world calls *Love*." Having been turned down (surprise, surprise), Whitefield finally married Elizabeth James, the woman whom Whitefield's friend Howell Harris loved, but whom, just for that reason, he thought he ought to surrender to a better man. (See A.

Dallimore, *George Whitefield*, 2 vols., [London: Banner of Truth, 1970, 1980], I.471, II 101-13.) John Wesley chose to marry a sour Huguenot widow whom he admired for "your indefatigable industry, your exact frugality, your uncommon neatness and cleanness both in your person, your clothes and all things round you": it was a disaster. (See John Pollock, *John Wesley* [Wheaton, Ill.: Victor, 1989], 210-12.) The loveless utilitarianism of these approaches to marriage is surely its own condemnation quite apart from the miseries to which it gave rise.

14. *A Christian Directory* (Morgan, Pa.: Soli Deo Gloria, 6th ed., 1996), 401-2.

15. *A Christian Directory*, 394-547. The "Appurtenances" are discussions of specific problems of right action ("cases of conscience") arising out of the generalized statements of "duties."

16. Arranged marriages, for the securing of property, wealth, and social standing, were common among seventeenth-century aristocrats and were totally approved by society.

17. "It is better to marry than to be aflame with passion" (NRSV).

18. *A Christian Directory*, 395.

19. *A Christian Directory*, 398.

20. *A Christian Directory*, 398-400.

21. *A Christian Directory*, 403.

22. *A Christian Directory*, 431.

23. *A Christian Directory*, 433.

24. *A Christian Directory*, 431-38.

25. *Practical Works of Richard Baxter*, IV.234: From *The Poor Man's Family Book* (1672). *A Christian Directory* was contained in vol. I of this set.

26. Daniel Rogers, *Matrimonial Honour* (1642), 148.

27. *A Christian Directory*, 401.

28. F. J. Powicke, *A Puritan Idyll, or the Reverend Richard Baxter's Love Story* (Manchester, 1918: reprinted from *Bulletin of the John Rylands Library*, 4); Lloyd-Thomas; Wilkinson.

29. Wilkinson, 19; Lloyd-Thomas, 268; F. J. Powicke, *The Reverend Richard Baxter Under the Cross*, 101.

30. Keeble, 127; see 121-31.

31. 139.

32. They are in Wilkinson, 62-65.

33. Wilkinson, 65.

34. 57.

35. 100.

36. 56.

37. 77.

38. 84.
39. 84.
40. 76.
41. 95-96.
42. Lloyd-Thomas, 270-71. The quotation from Margaret is on II.## 36 below. It is an almost verbatim echo of sentences in *The Saints' Everlasting Rest* (1649; 802), "suggesting that Margaret seems to have known passages of Baxter's writing so well as to quote from memory" (Wilkinson, 85). That does not, of course, make it any the less Margaret's own sentiment.
43. Baxter regularly sent his parishioners letters when communicating matters of permanent spiritual significance to which he and they would need to refer in the future. Baxter's solution to the problem of keeping copies of significant letters in that pre-carbon paper, pre-photocopier, pre-computer age was to ask for his letter back after its contents had been noted, and copied if the recipient so wished. This explains Margaret's transcribings, which Baxter reproduces.
44. 89.
45. 94.
46. Lloyd-Thomas, 271-72.
47. *Poetical Fragments* (1681) (facsimile reprint, Farnborough: Gregg, 1971), "The Epistle to the Reader."
48. *Poetical Fragments.*
49. *Poetical Fragments*, 65-74, 75-80, 81-83, 102-19. The three-part poem, "The Complaint—the Answer—the Submission," 89-96, and "The Return," 96-102, might well also owe their origin to Margaret's spiritual struggles. The familiar hymn that begins, "Lord, it belongs not to my care / Whether I die or live," is taken from "The Covenant and Confidence of Faith."
50. 151-56.
51. *A Treatise of Conversion* (1657), the printed version of the sermons Margaret heard, is in *Practical Works of Richard Baxter*, II.## 397-500. Two more publications on the same topic, *A Call to the Unconverted* (1658) and *Directions and Persuasions to a Sound Conversion* (1658), appear to have started life as courses of sermons; Margaret would have heard them too. They are in *Practical Works* II.## 501-44, 580-661.
52. 101. Richard had stipulated this surrender "so that I be not entangled in lawsuits." There was a wrangle in the late 1650s between Francis Charlton, Margaret's brother and heir to the Apley estate, and Mrs. Hanmer, who had declined to free him from his debts by giving him money that his father had intended for Margaret and her sister Mary. Francis believed that Richard had

unduly influenced Mrs. Hanmer in her decision, and no doubt Richard
feared that now Mrs. Hanmer was dead Francis might sue Margaret for the
money in question. See Wilkinson, 23-26, and N.H. Keeble and G.F.
Nuttall, *Calendar of the Correspondence of Richard Baxter* (Oxford:
Clarendon Press, 1991), no. 464, I.318. Notwithstanding the surrender, she
remained "well-to-do" (G.F. Nuttall, *Richard Baxter* [London: Thomas
Nelson, 1965], 94).

53. 128-29.

54. 146.

55. 141. "Though she oft said that before she married me she expected more
sourness and unsuitableness than she found; yet I am sure that she found less
zeal and holiness and strictness in all words and looks and duties, and less
help for her soul, than she expected." 131-32.

56. Lloyd-Thomas, 249.

57. II.## 66.

58. Though Richard here and on page 52 calls Margaret's condition melancholy
(roughly corresponding to clinical depression in our vocabulary), no doubt
because she herself so regarded it, he diagnoses it on page 49 as being rather
"a partly natural partly adventitious diseased fearfulness in a tender over-
passionate nature, that had no power to quiet her own fears, without any
other cloud on her understanding." The criterion of true melancholy in
Baxter's thinking was that it impeded rational thought and hence receptivity
to rational counseling. This was never Margaret's case.

59. 119-20.

60. *Poetical Fragments*, "The Epistle to the Reader."

61. 128.

62. 135.

63. 136.

64. 135.

65. 123.

66. 123.

67. 104-05.

68. 104.

69. 142.

70. 149.

71. Keeble, 131.

Part II
Great Goodness

1. Keeble, 127-31. The quotation is from pg. 129.
2. In 1659. See note below.
3. Baxter apparently refers here to Margaret's fostering care of his great-nephew William Baxter and her generosity to others of his own "poor kindred"; see Powicke, *The Reverend Richard Baxter Under the Cross*, chapter six, 109-27. "She was much more liberal to many of my own poor kindred than I was" (below, ## 44).
4. In chapter seven, "Of Her Exceeding Desires to Do Good."
5. Thomas Wright, "a man of extraordinary learning, ability, moderation, and peaceableness," was ejected in 1662 from the parish of Kynersly in Shropshire (*Reliquiae Baxterianae* [RB] III.94).
6. Henry Hickman was a fellow of Magdalen College, Oxford, ejected in 1662.
7. Baxter's *Treatise of Conversion* (1657) consisted of "some plain sermons on that subject, which Mr. Baldwin (an honest young minister that had lived in my house, and learned my proper [personal] characters of short-hand in which I wrote my sermon-notes) had transcribed out of my notes" (*RB* I.114).
8. Jackson was the physician whom Baxter persuaded to settle in Kidderminster, previously physicianless. Bates was a physician whom Baxter consulted about his own health, and who later became personal physician to Charles II. Prujean is not known.
9. Baxter arranged for Margaret to stay for a time with Richard Foley at Stourbridge: see 131 below, and note 43.
10. Baxter tried many new and to us strange remedies for his chronic bad health. In this case, "having read in Dr. Gerhard the admirable effects of the swallowing of a gold bullet upon his own father in a case like mine, I got a gold bullet and swallowed it ... and having taken it, I knew not how to be delivered of it again. I took clysters [enemas] and purges for about three weeks, but nothing stirred it.... But at last my neighbors set a day apart to fast and pray for me, and I was freed from my danger at the beginning of that day" (*RB* I.81).
11. One of the four times can be identified with fair certainty: an attack of smallpox. The sacking by Parliamentary troops of her stepfather's home, Apley Castle, when "men lay killed before her face" and she was among the family members "threatened and stripped of their clothing" (below, ## 49), was not apparently one of the four: see ## 69 below.
12. Baxter's interpolation.

13. "Friend" is a correction of "friends" in the printed text, which is almost certainly a misprint occasioned by "friends" three lines above. Puritans taught that each Christian needs a "bosom-friend" (a "soul friend," as some modern Christians would say), to whom one opens one's heart in an accountability relationship. Margaret calls Baxter "my dear friend" because he was fulfilling this role in her life.

14. This echo of Hebrews 4:9 probably shows that Margaret had fed her soul on Baxter's best-selling *Saints' Everlasting Rest,* a treatise based on this text. Some of the preceding sentences are almost verbatim quotations from Baxter's book.

15. 1660.

16. 1660.

17. The reference is to Baxter.

18. Baxter.

19. Apley Castle, near Wellington, Shropshire.

20. "The procedure in England for getting married consisted of (1) espousals, a contract to marry corresponding to the modern engagement, but more binding, inasmuch as sexual relations with a third party during the espousal period were classed as adultery; (2) publication of the banns (an announcement that the contract exists) on three successive Sundays in church; (3) execution of the espousal contract by vows of entry into actual marriage, taken before witnesses as part of a special service" (J.I. Packer, *A Quest for Godliness: The Puritan Vision of the Christian Life* [Wheaton, Ill.: Crossway, 1990], 268-69). Samuel Clark, a friend of Baxter and compiler of several volumes of Christian biography, in the last of which a summary of the Breviate was included, was ejected in 1662 and died in 1682. Simeon Ash, who died in 1662 just before he would have been ejected, "was one of our oldest nonconformists,... a Christian of the primitive simplicity ... of a holy life, of a cheerful mind, and of a fluent elegancy in prayer" (*RB* II.430). Henry Ashurst was a well-to-do Christian layman, an alderman of the City of London and another of Baxter's personal friends.

21. Morley was the newly consecrated bishop of the restored Worcester diocese, in which Kidderminster was situated.

22. Baxter refers to the Five-Mile Act of 1665, which required Nonconforming clergy to reside at least five miles from any population center "that sent Burgesses to the Parliament," or any place where they themselves had once had a ministry, and to take an oath of loyalty to the crown and to the status quo in church and state. Under this Act Baxter suffered a brief imprisonment in 1669, after which he left Acton for Totteridge.

23. The Declaration of Indulgence, 1672.

24. Unsanitary inner London was never good for Baxter's fragile health. Southampton Square (the modern Bloomsbury Square) was however outside the city wall, northeast of St. Giles-in-the-Fields, with open country all around.

25. The modern St. Martin's-in-the-Fields.

26. When Baxter was preaching at St. Dunstan's-in-the-West in 1661, "a little lime and dust (and perhaps a piece of a brick or two) fell down in the steeple or belfry" and caused panic in the congregation for fear the church was collapsing (*RB* II.301-2).

27. One evening in James I's reign a Jesuit, Father Drury, was preaching at Blackfriars, London, in an upstairs room when the floor fell and ninety-four persons plus the preacher died. The accident was named the Fatal Vespers.

28. Coventry was secretary to the King, i.e., Secretary of State. The modern Coventry Street in which he lived is named after him.

29. Rector of St. Martin's.

30. Probably the catechism in the Anglican Prayer Book; possibly the Westminster Shorter Catechism, which Baxter had used in his Kidderminster ministry.

31. Thomas Gouge, who died in 1681, was "a wonder of sincere industry in works of charity." Baxter notes, after Gouge's ejection from his London parish (St. Sepulchre's) in 1662, "his conjunction with Alderman Ashurst and some such others, in a weekly meeting, to take account of the honest poor families in the city that were in great want;... his voluntary catechizing the Christ's Church boys when he might not preach; the many thousand Bibles printed in Welsh that he dispersed in Wales," along with thousands of other books given out free; "his setting up about 300 or 400 schools in Wales to teach children only to read, and the catechism; his industry to beg money for all this, besides most of his own estate laid out on it; his travels over Wales once or twice a year to visit his schools:... this was true episcopacy of a silenced minister" (*RB* III.190).

32. Thomas Manton (1620-77) was a prolific Puritan preacher of Baxter's type, who with Baxter shared in the leadership group of "mere nonconformists," incorrectly dubbed Presbyterians, at and after the Restoration (1660).

33. "Sergeant" in Baxter's day designated the highest rank of lawyers. John Fountaine was a godly well-wisher who gave Baxter legal advice and an annual gift of ten pounds sterling from 1662 on until his death in 1671 (*RB* III.86).

34. Sir Thomas Davis was "an Alderman Justice ... who understood not the law, but was ready to serve the prelates [bishops] in their own way" (*RB* III.165). In 1675 he fined Baxter sixty pounds for preaching two sermons,

specifying that the fine should be paid by confiscation and sale of the preacher's possessions.

35. "In good faith," that is, as a genuine gift, not a secret arrangement whereby Baxter could get his books back at a later date. He gave Harvard library "some of my Commentaries and some Historians" (Powicke, 88ff.).

36. Writers on medical and dietetic matters. Cornarius (Cornario) was Professor of Medicine at Marburg and Jena in the mid-sixteenth century.

37. That is, such actions and words, when not appropriately used for expressing the true desires of a godly heart, are not actually righteousness and prayer.

38. The reader was the leader in the exercises of worship before the preaching. The chapters were the Scripture portions set for the day in the Prayer Book lectionary. Since none of the items listed involved wording peculiar to the Prayer Book, Baxter could fairly claim that he was not using the book liturgically, even though Psalms, Creed, Decalogue, and Lord's Prayer were included in the set services.

39. Richard Foley was a wealthy landowner, Worcestershire dignitary, and Christian philanthropist, who in 1638 had arranged for Baxter to be ordained despite his lack of a university degree, so that he might head up the school Foley was founding in Dudley. He and his son Thomas were lifelong friends to Baxter, who was thus able to arrange for his sick parishioner to stay at Foley's home.

40. "The [Civil] wars being ended, and she as guardian possessing her son's estate, took him (an only son) as herself [i.e., identified herself with his interests], and used his estate as carefully as for herself, but out of it conscientiously paid debts of her husband's, repaired some of the ruined houses, and managed things faithfully, according to her best discretion, until her son, marrying, took his estate into his own hands" (Breviate, ed. J.T. Wilkinson, 68). Mother and son (Francis) were already estranged over Mrs. Hanmer's management of the estate: see ## 15, note ## 52, above.

41. This letter dates from 1665, the Plague year, when Baxter spent some time as a guest of his friend Richard Hampden at the latter's country seat in Hampden (today, Great Hampden), Buckinghamshire. See Keeble and Nuttall, no. 726, II.47-48.

42. "The romance invented by Titus Oates and Israel Tonge in August 1678, of a Jesuit conspiracy to kill Charles and enthrone his brother [James, afterward James II, a declared Roman Catholic] by armed rebellion, focused on one centre all the random germs of anti-popery that had been circulating in the English political system for generations" (J.P. Kenyon, *The Stuarts* [London: Fontana, 1966], 127). Rumors of "popish plots" and planned uprisings, framed by the knowledge that the proper heir to the throne was a robust Romanist, kept England on tenterhooks for the next few years.

43. Baxter was something of an expert on "melancholy," which to him meant a depressed condition in which coherent and logical thought about one's own condition becomes impossible. "Clinical depression" would be our label for it. The "doleful evils" he refers to are the compulsive urgings toward despairing, self-destructive behavior and suicide that afflict persons thus depressed.

44. Sir Matthew Hale, Oliver Cromwell's Lord Chief Justice, was Baxter's neighbor at Acton, and they became good friends. "Hale tolerated Baxter's preaching in his own [Baxter's] home, and his testimony on Baxter's behalf was instrumental in securing his release when these conventicles led to his imprisonment in June 1669. For his part, Baxter was won by Hale's remarkable sagacity, erudition, strictness of life, unostentatious manner, humility, and, above all, his soundness of judgment and integrity" (Keeble, 127). In 1676 Baxter wrote, having noted that Hale seemed to be terminally ill: "It is not the least of my pleasure that I have lived some years in his more than ordinary love and friendship, and that we are now waiting which shall be first in heaven; whither, he saith, he is going with full content and acquiescence in the will of a gracious God, and doubts not but we shall shortly live together" (*RB* III.176).

Part III
Great Sadness

1. Annual Report of Ontario Bible College and Ontario Theological Seminary, 1995-96, 5.

2. *Christians Grieve Too,* Donald Howard (Edinburgh: Banner of Truth, 1980).

3. C.S. Lewis, *A Grief Observed* (New York: Bantam, 1976), 1, 3-4. "And grief still feels like fear. Perhaps, more strictly, like suspense. Or like waiting; just hanging about waiting for something to happen. It gives life a permanently provisional feeling. It doesn't seem worth starting anything. I can't settle down. I yawn, I fidget, I smoke too much" (38-39).

4. *Poetical Fragments,* "To the Reader." See 100 above. The "wise friends" advised him not to publish *Poetical Fragments.*

5. 56 above.

6. *A Grief Observed,* 65.

7. *A Grief Observed,* 68-69.

8. *A Grief Observed,* 71-72.

9. For details, see biographies of Lewis. George Sayer, *Jack*, 2d ed., with "Afterword" (Wheaton, Ill.: Crossway, 1994), is certainly the best.

10. 56, 138.

11. N.H. Keeble, *Richard Baxter, Puritan Man of Letters*, 128, quoting John Howe, *A Godly Pattern for All Women*, 1681, 40. "I hope her example more fully and publicly represented, will more generally teach," ibid., 41.

12. 138.

13. 149.

14. Lloyd-Thomas, 249.

15. 57.

16. 149.

17. Lloyd-Thomas, 8-9, 237-38. Richard's chronic bad health is reflected in these lines from the autobiographical poem, "Love Breathing Thanks and Praise," relating to his early ministry:

> Still thinking I had little time to live,
>
> My fervent heart to win men's souls did strive.
>
> I preached, as never sure to preach again,
>
> And as a dying man to dying men. (*Poetical Fragments*, 40.)

18. See on this J.I. Packer, "Richard Baxter on Heaven, Hope and Holiness," in J.I. Packer and Loren Wilkinson, eds., *Alive to God: Studies in Spirituality* (Downers Grove, Ill., and Leicester, U.K.: InterVarsity Press, 1992), 161-75.

19. 137.

20. Keeble, 129.

21. Lloyd-Thomas, 249.

22. 139.

23. 140-41.

24. 141, 142, 143.

25. Prayers in the home, twice daily.

26. 120-21.

27. *A Grief Observed*, 55-56.

28. 126.

29. 126.

30. 125.

31. 125-26.

32. 136.

33. 126.

34. 129.

35. 126.

36. 136.
37. 141.
38. 120.
39. 144.
40. 118.
41. 101.
42. 145.
43. 121.
44. 123.
45. 118-19.
46. 145.
47. 101.
48. *A Grief Observed*, 89.
49. 136-37.
50. 148-49.
51. *A Grief Observed*, 83-84.
52. 134.
53. 131-32.